Books by Peter Barnes

Out of Darkness into Light
The Trinity

The Watchtower

in Light of Scripture

PETER BARNES

CHALLENGE MINISTRIES
www.challengemin.org

The Watchtower
in Light of Scripture

Cover design: Jerry Benson

First printing, 2003

Printed in the United States of America

ISBN 0-9747009-0-8

Introduction

The foundation of this book is a collection of audio tapes recorded over the years by Peter Barnes on various teachings of the Jehovah's Witnesses. Although the format has changed somewhat, we have attempted to keep some of the same "feel" of a speaker before a live audience. The idea was to capture a more personal instruction of a teacher decipling a friend. You might even hear Peter's English accent come through from time to time.

David Costantino had the idea of assembling Peter's tapes and converted them to a digital format. Lori Necochea and Jerry Benson assisted Peter in the editing process. Jerry Benson also typeset the book and did the cover artwork.

The chapters that follow are examples of fundamental teachings of the religious organization, the *Watchtower Bible and Tract Society*. The Watchtower's followers, known as the Jehovah's Witnesses, arrive at particular beliefs directed by the "organization" that contradict Scripture. As Christians, we are more effective in ministering to these lost people if we familiarize ourselves with their false doctrine. The Watchtower's teachings have led the Jehovah's Witnesses into confusion and darkness. If we are prepared to respond to their false teachings, we expose the darkness of the Watchtower while evangelizing the Truth in Light of Scripture.

Here's a brief introductory letter by Peter.

My Dear Friends,

I was an active member of Jehovah's Witnesses for thirty years, from the spring of 1949 to December 1978. In that period I went from door to door in many local communities endeavoring to spread the Watchtower message. For thirty years I strove to serve God while being in a condition of severe spiritual darkness.

The apostle Paul in his second letter to the Corinthian Church provides us with a perfect description of the spiritual condition of people such as Jehovah's Witnesses:

> And even if our gospel is veiled, it is veiled to those who are perishing, in whose case the god of this world has blinded the minds of the unbelieving, that they might not see the light of the gospel of the glory of Christ, who is the image of God. 2 Cor 4:3-4 NASB

But, in His own due time, the Lord Jesus Christ had mercy on me and opened my eyes to the truth of the gospel and I have been praising and thanking God ever since. I look forward to serving the Lord Jesus Christ for the rest of my life on earth and throughout eternity to come. I will never cease to thank and praise our triune God (Father, Son and Holy Spirit) for His wonderful work of Grace towards me.

Peter Barnes

Phil 3:7-10

Contents

Chapter 1

Prophecy

The following chapters are examples of the fundamental teachings of the religious organization, the *Watchtower Bible and Tract Society*. The Watchtower's followers, known as Jehovah's Witnesses, arrive at particular beliefs that contradict Scripture. As Christians we are more effective in ministering to these lost people if we familiarize ourselves with their false doctrine. The Watchtower's teachings have led the Jehovah's Witnesses into confusion and darkness. If we are prepared to respond to their false teachings, we expose the darkness of the Watchtower while evangelizing the Truth in light of Scripture.

The theme of this chapter is "False Prophets". Therefore, we're going to define what a false prophet is according to Scripture. We will also decide whether or not Jehovah's Witnesses are false prophets. I would like to begin with the Gospel of Matthew 7:15-23. We'll analyze some of the points that are made in the passages keeping in mind that these are the words of our Lord Himself. This is His discussion on the topic of false prophets, and it begins in verse 15. Jesus is speaking to the people:

> Beware of false prophets who come to you in sheep's clothing, but inwardly are ravenous wolves. You will know them by their fruits. Grapes are not gathered from thorn bushes nor figs from thistles, are they? Even so, every good tree bears good fruit, but the bad tree bears bad fruit. A good tree cannot produce bad fruit, nor can a bad tree produce good fruit. Every tree that does not bear good fruit is cut down and thrown into the fire. So then you will know them by their fruits. Not everyone, who says to me, Lord, Lord, will enter into the kingdom of heaven, but he who does the will of my Father who is in heaven. Many will say to me in that day, Lord, Lord, did we not

> prophesy in your name and in your name cast out de-
> mons and in your name perform many miracles? And
> then I will declare to them, I never knew you. Depart
> from Me, you who practice lawlessness.

What a powerful statement! Jesus said, "Beware of false prophets." The word "beware" is a very strong word. It means that you are to be on the alert. We must be prepared to defend ourselves against spiritual danger. That's all inherent and implicit in the word, "beware."

Jesus is obviously saying to believers, 'Hey, listen, don't be complacent about these false prophets.' Don't go on your merry little way as a Christian and let the false prophets go on their merry little way. Don't pretend that they're not there and be like an ostrich and stick your head in the sand and maybe it'll go away. Jesus said to the Christian, "beware".

We need to know the problem of the false prophets. Jesus said, "beware of the false prophets who come to you". Isn't that interesting? That's rather intriguing, because out of all the religions in Christendom, there are two organizations above all others who go out of their way to come to you. One of them is the Mormon Church, which sends its missionaries out. The other is Jehovah's Witnesses. They are the very ones who make a big feature of coming to you, so the Scripture says beware of false prophets who come to you in sheep's clothing.

Immediately we see that particular metaphor being used. Jesus is talking about the analogy of Himself as the Shepherd and His followers, His disciples, as being little sheep. Jesus is the Good Shepherd who leads the sheep into the sheepfold and to eternal life to inherit the King-dom. But He warns false prophets come to you in sheep's clothing. They have an outward identification that when you look at them and listen to them, you would at first think that they are the sheep. They appear to be true disciples of the Shepherd, Christ.

But in reality, inwardly, you can't see this. You can't detect it by outward observation, but inwardly, they are what? They are ravenous wolves. Now, of course, Jesus is applying this in a spiritual sense. He means just as a hungry wolf (and the word "ravenous", by the way, means to be very hungry and ready to kill). So, in a spiritual sense, they are eager to devour you spiritually. The false prophet will come to you and ruin your spiritual life. They will make a mess of it for you therefore you must beware.

That's a pretty strong statement in verse 15. But what's He hinting at when He says you will know them by their fruits? I want to suggest to you, my friends, that we don't read into that passage more than is there. We know that the New Testament writers have a lot to say about the "fruits of the Spirit". But you see this isn't particularly what Jesus is referring to in this passage. He's talking about the fruits of prophetic utterances. He's talking about the work of prophets, and He says you'll know these false prophets by their fruits. Grapes are not gathered from thorn bushes, and figs are not gathered from thistles, are they?

In other words, He's saying you can't get good wholesome prophetic statements out of these false prophets. This is impossible because to get a good prophetic statement out of them would be like getting a fig tree to produce a thistle. It just doesn't work. It's against the natural order. In verse 17, He says every good tree bears good fruit, and the bad tree bears bad fruit.

Therefore, those who truly are appointed as prophets of God are going to have wholesome and valuable prophetic utterances to make for the benefit of the people. Those who are false prophets are going to have the bad prophetic utterances that are dangerous and detrimental.

Verse 18, says, "A good tree cannot produce bad fruit; nor can a bad tree produce good fruit." In other words, if you were a true prophet of God, there is no way that you're going to make a false prophetic utterance. It will never happen. On the other hand, if you're actually a false prophet, you will never make a true prophetic utterance. You're incapable of doing it.

Furthermore, Jesus goes on to show what the results are going to be for the false prophets. Although these consequences will not come (verse 21) until the Day of Judgment, at that time these false prophets will try to acknowledge Jesus as their Lord. Jesus says that they will come and exclaim, "Did we not prophesy in your name?" That's one of the claims - they're obviously claiming to be prophets. Verse 23 - Jesus responds, "I will declare to them - (now note this very carefully) - I never knew you."

Jesus didn't say to these false prophets, "Well, you know at one time I knew you, but then I had to kind of wash My hands of you." He didn't say that. He said, "I never knew you." You were never one of Mine. You never belonged to Me, and I never sanctioned anything that you did." So therefore, "depart from Me, you who practice lawlessness." They were actually breakers of the laws of God.

The situation for a false prophet is very serious. This isn't something to take lightly. We're going to see that many Jehovah's Witnesses do try and take it lightly and treat it as if it's no big deal at all.

Let's get the definition then of a false prophet and false prophecy from the Book of Deuteronomy 18:20. Almighty God speaking to the people, "The prophet who shall speak words presumptuously in My name which I have not commanded him to speak or which he shall speak in the name of other gods, that prophet shall die."

Obviously we're seeing two things - that a false prophet is one who either speaks in the name of false gods or even dares to speak in the name of the true God. But he's speaking, presumptuously, words that the true God did not tell him to speak. Look at the results. That prophet shall die. It's a death sentence on that prophet.

The Jehovah's Witness Bible, the *New World Translation* reads in verse 21:

> And in case you should say in your heart, how shall
> we know the word that Jehovah has not spoken? When
> the prophet speaks in the name of Jehovah and the word
> does not occur or come true that is the word that Jehovah
> did not speak. With presumptuousness, the prophet spoke
> it.

Of course in their Bible, it uses the name Jehovah. Remember that Jehovah's Witnesses are the only organized group in the whole world who come and speak to you in the name of Jehovah. They're the only ones that have officially claimed to do that. So their Bible, then, is very appropriate for them, isn't it? Because it says if they come and they speak the word of Jehovah and it doesn't come true, then they have spoken presumptuously words that Jehovah did not give them to speak.

There is no doubt that Jehovah's Witnesses claim to be God's prophet for today. They have made many such claims in their literature over the years, but we'll concentrate on an article published in the April 1, 1972 edition of the *Watchtower* magazine, page 197.

The article commences with the heading, "They Shall Know that a Prophet Was Among Them." The use of the word "They" in the heading is a reference to the people of the churches of Christendom - all the religious people that go to church is what the article refers to as "They". These church people, these religionists, are going to know what was among them? A prophet was among them.

According to the Watchtower leaders, the Christians in these churches will suddenly realize that there was a prophet in their midst. Guess who the prophet is? Who is he going to turn out to be? Is it going to be Uncle Ebeneezer? Is it going to be old mother Shipton? Is it going to be Jeanne Dixon? No! The article continues;

> So, does Jehovah have a prophet to help them? Will
> this prophet warn them of dangers? Will this prophet de-
> clare things to come?

That sounds like the work of a prophet, doesn't it? He will declare things to come. That's the work of a prophet.

In the article the question is raised: 'Who is this prophet?' " This prophet was not one man but was a body of men and women." So we notice they're claiming that they don't have just one person whom they point to as the prophet, but rather, a group or a body of men and women identified as the "prophet" for the organization.

The article goes on to identify them. It says it was a small group of footstep followers of Jesus known at that time; (and they're talking about an earlier time in their history) known as the *International Bible Students*. That was the name of Jehovah's Witnesses before they took this particular name. Judge Rutherford gave them the name, Jehovah's Witnesses, in the year 1931. Rutherford was the President of the *Watchtower* Society in those days.

Therefore it means that from 1870 to 1931, a period of at least 60 to 61 years they were known as the *International Bible Students*. And then they took on the new name. It goes on in the paragraph to say, "today they are known as Jehovah's Christian Witnesses." By the way, that's not true. They are not known as Jehovah's Christian Witnesses. They are known simply as Jehovah's Witnesses.

Go to the nearest Kingdom Hall and see what it says. It will say Kingdom Hall of Jehovah's Witnesses. The word Christian isn't there.

Are they claiming to be a prophet or are they not? Isn't this clear enough? The final paragraph states,

> Of course it's easy to say that this group acts as a prophet of God. It's another thing to prove it. The only way that this can be done is to review the record. What does it show?

And I say amen to that. Let's put them to the test. They have given us the invitation. Let's review the record. Is that fair? Yes, I think it is.

In 1889 the book is called, *The Time Is At Hand*. It was a book published by Charles Russell the founder of the International Bible Students (Jehovah's Witnesses). It was part of the series, the *Studies in the Scriptures*. On Page 101 of the 1908 edition, it said:

> The battle of the great day of God Almighty, which is mentioned in Revelation 16:14 which will end in A.D. 1914 with the complete overthrow of earth's present rulership has already commenced.

Russell was referring to the Battle of Armageddon mentioned in the 16th chapter of Revelation. Russell is saying, hey listen, I'm telling you guys that that battle is already on. It's already started way back here, and it was written in 1889. He's saying that the battle is started. And guess what, it is going to come to it's finish, and it's going to result in the complete overthrow of the governments of the present earth in 1914.

Unbelievably, that's exactly what it says. There's no getting around it. There's no sidestepping it. Russell believed and prophesied that the total end of the Age was coming in 1914, and it would see the complete overthrow of all the governments of the earth, and in actual fact would see their replacement by the government of Jesus Christ and the 144,000. That's what they actually have taught, and that's what Russell prophesied.

Now, did that happen? No, of course it didn't. If it did, then I don't know where I was because I didn't notice it. Maybe I had been on my vacation or something, but I didn't see it. You know, it tends to make you feel a little sarcastic about it, because it's such a blatant wrong; such blatant error - it's incredible.

In 1897, this is the series, *Studies in the Scriptures*, and it's volume 4, page 621 says, "Our Lord, the appointed King (and that's in reference to Jesus) is now present since October of 1874." What did Russell mean by that? He's saying we all know and we all believe that the Bible teaches the Second Coming of Christ has already occurred. Russell is saying Christ has already come back. Russell is using the word "present", isn't he?

He says that our King is now present, and He's been present here with us since October of 1874. And that's another thing that Russell believed and prophesied about - that the invisible return of the Lord was due to take place in the year 1874. Well now, was that a true prophecy? If you say to a Jehovah's Witness when he comes to your doorstep, "I saw a reference to one of your early publications from the 1880s just a few days ago, and it said that Jesus actually returned invisibly to this earth in 1874, is that true? What do you think a Jehovah's Witness would say? He'd say, no - no, no, no, that's not true.

So you say, well, when did Jesus come back? The Jehovah's Witness would say he came back in 1914. So right there they would admit openly that Russell made a false prophecy. At the same time, they would probably try to deny such a prophecy was made. They would explain that you misunderstood it or you read it out of context, or it's a counterfeit publication or something like that. But nevertheless, it's there, and I have the original books to back that up and to prove it if it's needed.

Let's consider 1918. I should tell you, by the way, that in 1916 Charles Russell died, and his position as a false prophet came to an end right there. The hand of death stilled the voice of that false prophet, and Joseph Rutherford took his place the next year, 1917. Now what was Rutherford going to do?

In 1918, the publication entitled, *Millions Now Living Will Never Die* was given as a public talk in the year 1918, and then it was put into print in the year 1920 and circulated millions of copies. Let me quote from page 89.

> Therefore, we may confidently expect that 1925 will mark the return of Abraham, Isaac, Jacob, and the prophets of old, particularly those named in Hebrews 11, to the condition of human perfection.

Now here's Rutherford setting himself up as a prophet for the people. He's prophesying to millions of people and having it published in this book, *Millions Now Living Will Never Die*, to the tune of millions of copies for distribution all over the United States and Europe. In it he's saying that 1925 is going to mark the return of Abraham, Isaac, and Jacob from the dead - that they're going to be resurrected that year. I have to ask you, did that happen? Did anybody see a man with a long, white beard down to his toes walking around and saying, "Hey, fellows, I'm Abraham. Don't you realize I'm Abraham?" No, of course you haven't. You didn't back in 1925 either, because neither Abraham nor Isaac nor Jacob put in an appearance from the dead.

In fact, we are now in the year 2003, I believe, and if my mathematics is any good, I make that to be 78 years after 1925. Would I be right, all you mathematicians? So we've gone beyond the date 1925 now by 78 years, and guess what? I'm telling you confidently that Abraham, Isaac, and Jacob still haven't come back from the dead. So that prophecy is slightly wrong.

In 1923, the Watchtower, first of that year, page 106 instructed the society with new prophetic utterances. The magazine stated, "Our thought is that 1925 is definitely settled by the Scriptures," and then Rutherford compares Noah with the Jehovah's Witnesses in the 1925 period. He says, "As to Noah, the Christian (he means the Jehovah's Witness) has much more upon which to base his faith than Noah had upon which to base his faith in the coming deluge."

Wow, Almighty God had spoken directly to Noah, had he not? And Almighty God Himself had told Noah that there was going to be a flood and instructed Noah to build this enormous ark for the preservation of his family and for specimens of the animals. So Noah had plenty to base his faith on; and yet the Watchtower leaders are saying, 'Hey, we Jehovah's Witnesses, we've gotten even more proof than Noah had on which to base our confidence in 1925.'

Can you hear the false prophets speaking? Can you catch the swelling pride and the puffed up words coming out of the mouth of the false prophets? But then in 1925, when the actual year arrived, the picture changed a little bit. Look at this quote from the *Watchtower* of January 1, 1925. "The year 1925 is here. With great expectation, Christians look forward to this year." Why? Because their false prophet has been hammering it across to them. "Many have confidently expected that all the members of the Body of Christ will be changed to heavenly glory (that means all their 144,000) this year. This may be accomplished." They profess this teaching with such confidence. But wait a minute. What's that? "It may not be?" Do I detect a slightly negative note from the great false prophet?" It may not be.

> "In his own due time, God will accomplish His purpose concerning His people. Christians should not be so deeply concerned about what may transpire this year."

Isn't that incredible? Talk about double talking and backtracking and all the rest of it. This is the typical jargon of a false prophet, you see? They play tightrope games with words. That's exactly what they're doing.

Finally, let's look at 1931. Now we have the book, *Vindication*, printed that year, page 338. Note this comment.

> There was a measure of disappointment on the part of Jehovah's faithful ones on earth concerning the years [*notice the dates*] 1914, 1918, and 1925, which disappointment lasted for a time, and they also learned to quit fixing dates.

Let me tell you something about that remark. That remark is the understatement of the century when it says it lead to some disappointment-there was a measure of disappointment which lasted for a time, the truth is peoples lives were shattered!

The lives of many Jehovah's Witnesses were ruined. Many Jehovah's Witnesses lost their faith in God completely.

Every time they got hooked on one of these dates and were all fired up, convinced that their true prophet of God had taught them truly, the dates came and went. They sincerely believed that God was going to act on those things that had been prophesied. The result however, was that nothing happened and the letdown was incredible. It was enormous, and thousands moved away from the Watchtower organization in total disappointment and complete disillusionment; and many of them never regained their faith in God again. Isn't that sad?

The next quote is even worse when it says; 'they also learned to quit fixing dates.' When I first read that, I thought they must have been talking recipes. You know what I mean, like date soufflé and fig truffle or whatever it is? (A little British humor.) But you see, what I'm getting at is that they did not learn to quit fixing dates on the calendar. Judge Rutherford went on to pinpoint 1941. When he died in 1942 the next Watchtower leader Nathan Knorr came on the scene and it wasn't many years before he was pinpointing 1975.

In 1968, the Watchtower of the 15th of August 1968, on page 494, with the entire article devoted the to question about why Jehovah's Witnesses are looking forward to 1975. In that article, they explain it's because 1975 is going to mark the end of 6,000 years of human history from Adam until the year 1975-exactly 6,000 years of Bible history. That should, logically, said the leaders of the Watchtower, be followed by the millennial kingdom, the reign of peace of Jesus. Therefore, all Jehovah's Witnesses zeroed in on that year, not just because it was the end of 6,000 years of human misery, but because they were confident that it was going to be the beginning of paradise for them and a release from all the misery of this world. That's what they really believed. And again, the letdown was absolutely enormous when nothing happened in the year 1975.

Let me tell you a little bit more about the 1975 fiasco. You see, I was a member of Jehovah's Witnesses at that time. I came into the Watchtower organization in 1949, and so by 1975, I had been with them for about 26 years. I was very carefully observing what was going on around the Kingdom Hall; and you couldn't imagine the excitement there was, especially in the year 1974. This was the final year before the showdown.

Jehovah's Witnesses' families had countdown calendars in their kitchens-especially designed calendars that they made themselves with all the months coming down to October of 1975. Nothing was on the calendar beyond that month because it all had to be over by then. That was the last deadline for it to happen. Isn't that amazing? And every month, the head of the family would go into the kitchen and religiously mark off another month and bring them closer and closer to the fateful deadline. It did turn out to be a fatal deadline, by the way, for many of them. And there were Jehovah's Witness elders who were family men and had wives and children to look after who were giving up their jobs and selling their homes and budgeting their money to last the family until October of 1975. Why? Because they weren't going to need money after that because the Kingdom of God would be fully established and they would be living on a paradise earth. Isn't that sad?

Let me tell you that according to the yearbooks of Jehovah's Witnesses, that they published themselves, in the following three years, '76, '77, and '78, Jehovah's Witnesses lost a total membership of a quarter of a million people. Think about it. I'll tell you, I've met some of those ex-Witnesses who left because of the failure of that '75 prophesy, and a more unhappy bunch of people you could never meet. Their faith is shattered. They are in a state of total disillusionment and they are in a spiritual limbo. The Watchtower leaders had poisoned their minds against the churches and they won't go near a church. They've lost their faith in that organization, so what's left for them?

This is the result of trusting in false prophecy. Remember what Jesus said in Matthew 7 that a bad tree cannot produce good fruit? The leaders of Jehovah's Witnesses have never made a true prophesy yet. They have got every single one of them wrong. And that's proving the words of Jesus as recorded in the Bible.

But now, what do the Jehovah's Witnesses themselves have to say about this bad state of affairs? Well, I'll tell you— and this is gleaned from experience in talking to dozens of them over the past few years. They have a list of excuses as long as your arm to try and cover up their position. I mean it. So I'm going to list them one by one.

Excuse No. 1 is, "We never claimed to be prophets." They will actually say that to you. So what do you do about that? Well, my friends, challenge them to go to their Kingdom Hall and get that 1972 *Watchtower*, because it's in their library in the Kingdom Hall. You know the best way to do it is to say to them 'According to a book I read, you did claim to be a prophet. This is what you said in that Watchtower. You claimed to be prophets.'

Now they will hem and haw and they will kind of look very suspicious. So you say, 'I'll tell you what, I wondered if this book is genuine myself. You can help me. Would you be prepared to go to your Kingdom Hall and actually turn to the Watchtower, which is quoted, and take that page and read it to yourself and see whether it's what is says here. And if it isn't come back and show me, and I will try and expose the people that made this as a lie.' Do you see the idea? Challenge them on it. You will find they don't want to do that. Oh no, they do not want to do that.

Excuse No. 2 is, "We never claimed to be inspired prophets." That's interesting. Think about that one. What's the difference between a Jehovah's Witness saying to you, "We never claimed to be prophets," or a Jehovah's Witness saying to you, "We never claimed to be *inspired prophets.*"

What's the difference? Now look, if he says we never claimed to be inspired prophets, what he means is, "Well, we were uninspired prophets." Doesn't he mean that? You can only go two ways with this. If you're going to be a prophet, either you're an inspired prophet or you're an uninspired prophet.

Well, ask him that. You say, 'Okay, if your leaders never claimed to be inspired prophets, then you must be telling me that they were uninspired prophets.' And you get them to agree to it. You say, "Well, the Bible only knows of two kinds of prophets. You have inspired prophets who always speak the truth, and you've got uninspired prophets who always tell lies." You see?

Then you ask, "So which one do you say you are now?" How foolish to say "we never claimed to be inspired prophets." The answer really is if you never claimed to be inspired prophets, then you should have shut your mouths and never had anything to say at all. That's what you should have done, because only the inspired prophets are entitled to open their mouths and speak on behalf of God.

Excuse No. 3: "Nobody is perfect. We all make mistakes. Even the apostles made mistakes." You know something? That's true. Nobody's perfect-yes, I would have to give a correct mark there. We all make mistakes - I would also have to give a correct mark there. Even the apostles made mistakes-I even have to give a correct mark there, but with a qualification.

When we look at the lives of the apostles as outlined in the Bible, we will see that at times they personally made mistakes. Peter made a whole bag load of them, didn't he? He told Jesus, confidently, just on the night of Christ's betrayal, he said, "I'll never betray you, Lord. I'll remain faithful unto death." And Jesus had to say, "Before the cock has crowed three times, you will have betrayed me three times."

Then later on when Peter was appointed as the apostle to the Jews he went out to the Galatian church. Peter fell into an erroneous act of conduct. The Galatian Church and the apostle Paul had to come and confront him in front of all the brothers and, and reprimand him and reprove him and set him straight. So, yes, they made personal mistakes. But, please notice the difference. Never did an inspired apostle of Jesus ever sit down and take his pen and put it to the parchment or the vellum or the papyrus and begin to write words on behalf of God in a letter to the Church and in the letter he makes a false prophesy. No apostle ever did that. Do you agree? Every word of every writing of every letter is totally true. The passages contain no error and contain no false prophecy..

But now, when we look at the mistakes of the leaders of Jehovah's Witnesses, we find not only have they opened their mouth in public broadcast, and broadcast to audiences of thousands their false prophecies, but they have sat down and taken pen to paper and have written out in minute detail their false prophecies. They have had them printed in their books, and the books have been published to millions by tens of millions of copies, and they have been circulated and distributed all over the world. They have commanded their followers to read and study these false prophecies and believe them. Don't tell me that's not true, because I was a Jehovah's Witness, and I studied those false prophecies; and I didn't dare not believe them, at least until I got my eyes opened. Do you see the point? So there's the difference. Don't you ever let a Jehovah's Witness get away with that silly excuse about 'nobody's perfect.'

Listen false prophets who give false prophecies are never forgiven in the Bible. Will you remember that little rule? God forgives all kinds of people for all kinds of things. There is never one word in the Holy Scripture about God forgiving or even being prepared to forgive a false prophet. Are you with me? Keep that in mind.

Okay, Excuse No. 4, "Our leaders apologized for their mistake." Oh, I love that one. By the way, after the failure of their 1975 prophecy, it took them 5 years to publish an apology. In the 1980 issue of The Watchtower they made a most miserable apology that you could ever imagine. It was an apology for an apology, if you know what I mean. It was really bad.

Now suppose they did apologize for their mistakes. I have to laugh about that one. Let's go back to Deuteronomy 18 and check your Bibles there. I suggest that you do this with Jehovah's Witnesses when you talk to them about their false prophecies. Remember in verse 21, "In case you should say in your heart, how should we know the word that Jehovah has not spoken?" Verse 22, "When the prophet speaks in the name of Jehovah, and the word doesn't occur, then that's the word that Jehovah did not speak. The prophet was presumptuous." Now, that's verse 22, isn't it?

I suggest that when they say 'Our leaders apologized,' you say 'Oh, you must be talking about that verse in the Bible in Deuteronomy, chapter 18, verse 23. Now, the Jehovah's Witness will probably not know what you're talking about. He will not be able to remember exactly what verse 23 says. But then you get him to look it up. He will turn and he will look and he will read, and he will say, "There's no verse 23 in my Bible." So you look him right in the eye, And you say, "Oh, are you sure you don't have a verse 23 that says something like 'Oh, and by the way, Jehovah says that if the false prophet apologizes for his false prophesy, everything is okay, and I will forgive him and everything in the garden is fine.'

Get the point? It will ram home to that Jehovah's Witness that there is nothing in the Bible where God makes allowances for people apologizing about their false prophecies, you see? So doing it that way, you can really get their attention and get your point across.

But we haven't finished with the list yet; we have Jonah, to consider. The Jehovah's Witnesses use passages from the Book of Jonah to show that righteous men in Scripture were false prophets. They will say, 'Well, it's no good you getting all hoity-toity with our leaders and accusing them of being false prophets. It can't be that big a deal, because after all Jonah was a false prophet, too. God allowed him to be his prophet and God allowed his Book of Jonah to be part of the inspired Bible. See? So we better go and look at the Book of Jonah, hadn't we, to see just exactly what he did whereby the Witnesses could brand him a false prophet.

So we go to Jonah, Chapter 3. Jonah has at last arrived at Nineveh. You remember first of all he tried to run away, and God wouldn't let him get away with that. He was determined that Jonah would go to the city of Nineveh and deliver God's message.

Let's take verse 1 of chapter 3. "Now the word of the Lord came to Jonah for the second time, saying arise and go to Nineveh, the great city, and proclaim to it the proclamation which I am going to tell you." Now, do you see that? God has definitely got a proclamation for Jonah to preach. Jonah isn't dreaming about the proclamation like the Watchtower leaders did or the false prophets, Jonah had his proclamation or prophecy given to him by the Lord God himself.

Verse 3, "So Jonah arose and went to Nineveh, according to the word of the Lord." Now Nineveh was an exceedingly great city, a three days' walk. Verse 4, "Then Jonah began to go through the city, one day's walk, and he cried out and said (now here's the prophecy that God gave him) "yet forty days and Nineveh will be overthrown." Notice, please, that Jonah did not say yet forty days and Nineveh might be overthrown, or Nineveh is in danger of being overthrown. Jonah said "Nineveh will be overthrown," and he got that message from God. Isn't that true? Isn't that what God told him to say? Yes. Jonah didn't change the message, but the truth is, and history testifies to the fact, that Nineveh did not get overthrown at that time. In fact, the city of Nineveh managed to continue on its existence for another 200 years or so after the time of Jonah. So what happened?

Jonah was given the message from the Almighty God Himself who never tells a lie and always speaks the truth. Jonah was a true prophet of God, and yet he gave a prophecy that didn't come true. My friends, it is very important to understand a fundamental principle, which we're now going to look at which governs the way God Himself operates towards people. Okay?

When Jonah uttered this pronouncement of doom, note the reaction of the Ninevites. Verse 6, when the word reached the king of Nineveh, he arose from his throne, laid aside his robe, covered himself with sackcloth and sat on ashes. He issued a proclamation, and it said:

> In Nineveh by the decree of the king and his nobles, do not man beast, herd, or flock taste a thing, do not let them eat or drink water, both man and beast must be covered with sackcloth, and let man call on God earnestly that each may turn from his wicked way and from the violence which is in his hands, and who knows, God may turn and relent and withdraw his burning anger so that we shall not perish.

It means that every last man of the Ninevites in this enormous city repented of their evil deeds before God in sackcloth and ashes. So what did God do? The next verse tells you. "When God saw their deeds that they turned away from their wicked ways, then God relented concerning the calamity with he declared that he would bring upon them, and He didn't do it." Are you ready for this? That's God's prerogative. This is grace triumphing over judgment, isn't it? Of course it is. And let me tell you the principle that runs all the way through the holy Bible, from beginning to end, that no matter how serious the sin, if there is true repentance on the part of the sinner, Almighty God, the Great Judge, will always forgive. Are you with me? So that's why the words of Jonah did not come true. It was nothing to do with him being a false prophet. It was the principle by which God Himself operates toward mankind.

Now, for Jehovah's Witnesses who want to liken themselves to Jonah and use that as an excuse for all their failed prophecies down through the years, it would mean that we would have to have a parallel situation. It would mean that when God sent His Jehovah's Witnesses to the people in 1914 to warn all the world of the end of the age in 1914, it didn't happen because the entire world repented in sackcloth and ashes. My friends, I don't believe they did. Do you? And then when they tried it again in 1918 and warned the world the second time and nothing happened, it would have to be because in 1918, the world got down on its knees and repented in sackcloth and ashes.

And then when they did it in 1925, down the world goes on its knees once more and repents, and so God had to keep on forgiving. It didn't happen that way, my friends. There is no comparison between the arrogant false prophecies of the Jehovah's Witnesses and the true prophecies of Jonah. Are you with me? So don't ever let them get away with that.

Their final excuse is amazing. Note this one. "Even if we are false prophets, I'm still not leaving Jehovah's organization, and I will tell you why." (This is based upon an amazing confrontation that I had a few years ago with a Jehovah's Witness man. This man personified the mindset and mental attitude of most Jehovah's Witnesses today.)

I went to this man's home. Somebody gave me his address. I didn't tell him who I was, and he didn't identify me. We got straight away into a discussion about Jehovah's Witnesses and false prophecy. I presented the man all the evidence that we've been sharing together in this chapter.

Now this young man (he was in his mid-thirties) had been a Jehovah's Witness all his life. He did not deny them. He didn't say 'Oh, that's not really a photocopy of the Watchtower.' He accepted it. He admitted it. He said that it was genuine. And I was able to go detail by detail from Pastor Russell's prophecies to Judge Rutherford's prophecies to Nathan Knorr's prophecies, and we looked at the whole thing. And in the end, this is what he said to me, "You've got me over a barrel there." You know what that means don't you? You've got them helpless. "But listen, I'm going to tell you why I don't think it matters, and I'm going to tell you why I am going to stay with Jehovah's Witnesses, even if we are false prophets." And here comes the list.

He said, "Number one, our organization is the only organization on the face of the earth that upholds and honors the divine name, Jehovah. Number two; we are the only persons who preach the good news of the Kingdom from door to door. Number three; we are the only persons who remain neutral in time of war. Number four; we're the only ones that uphold the sanctity of blood by not having blood transfusions. And Number 5, we're the only organization on the face of the earth that stays away from pagan holidays such as birthdays, Christmas, and Thanksgiving etc." And that was his list.

You know, it's like me going to somebody and saying, "Hey, fella, you're a murderer, and I can prove that you're a murderer, and here's the proof." And I show him all the documentary evidence, how many times he's murdered people, and he turns around and says to me, "You've got me over a barrel there. But I'll tell you I don't think it matters that I murdered a few people; because I love my wife. I'm good to my children, and I'm kind to dogs and other animals." Get the point? Listen. A murderer is a murderer, and a false prophet is a false prophet.

Chapter 2

New World Translation

This chapter will equip Christians to minister to the Jehovah's Witnesses and expose the misleading translation of God's Word they carry door to door. The Society is confident they use the most accurate interpretation of the original Greek and Hebrew transcripts. If you are going to engage in debate with Jehovah's Witnesses this information will enable you to show them things about their Bible that most Jehovah's Witnesses don't know about.

First of all, let me advise you about the background of the men who produced this "vaunted" *New World Translation* of the Bible. There was a group of five, who were all members of the governing body of Jehovah's Witnesses. However, their names do not appear anywhere in that Watchtower Bible. And not only that, if you write to the Watchtower headquarters in Brooklyn, New York, and request both the names and the academic credentials of the Watchtower translation committee, they will not supply that information to you.

Compare this with the Bible, the New American Standard, which was sponsored by the Lockman Foundation. It's true if you open up the covers of the NASB you won't find the names of the translation committee. However, if you write the Lockman Foundation requesting the list of names and the credentials of the translators, they'll send it to you. The list shows there's over 50 highly qualified men who are trained in Bible languages; and every one of them without exception has at least one Ph.D. in theology and Bible languages.

Definitely, the translators of the NASB are not trying to hide their qualifications. However, when it comes to the Watchtower translation committee, they come up with this fabulous excuse that they don't want to give the names of

these men so that all the glory for this wonderful translation will go solely to Jehovah God and not to these men. Of
course, you can't help thinking that there's a reverse side
to that coin. Doesn't this suggest that they also wish to remain anonymous so that nobody can actually point the finger at them because of what a bad translation it is? There's
always that side of it.

After spending 30 years as a former Jehovah's Witness, it is very obvious to me why the leaders of the Watchtower organization produced their own translation of the
Bible. There were many other good translations in existence at the time. The answer is that all the other leading
translations, which were available for use, fundamentally
contradicted the doctrines of the Jehovah's Witnesses in
many important areas. What it boiled down to was that the
Witness leaders wanted a Bible they could translate in such
a way that it would give virtually 100% support to their
particular way of interpreting the doctrines of Holy Scripture. I think that will become evident as we start going
through the information.

I'm going to use to a large extent the Kingdom Interlinear Translation of the Holy Scriptures produced by the
Watchtower Committee in 1969. First of all, I'm going to
refer to page 1158 in the Kingdom Interlinear Translation
(which I will call the KIT), page 1158 in the appendix under
John 1:1.

They comment on the Manual Grammar of the Greek
New Testament by professors Dana and Mantey. These two
men were very well known and were accepted as leading
authorities on Greek grammar throughout the world. Their
Greek manual has been very much used by Bible translators. It says:

> Careful translators recognize that the articular con-
> struction of the noun points to an identity, a personality,
> whereas an anarthrous construction points to a quality
> about someone.

All this is with reference to the last few words in John 1:1 which reads in the Watchtower Bible, "the Word was a god," instead of "the Word was God." The NWT translators are inferring that this Manual Grammar put out by professors Dana and Mantey really supports their interpretation. They go on to enlarge on the subject with an illustration of Dana and Mantey referring to a non-biblical Greek writing by a writer by the name of Xenothon. In his book, "Anabasis" he uses the example in the Greek language of "a marketplace". Dana and Mantey refer to the structure of the grammar in this Greek writing, which is correctly, they say translated as "a marketplace." Notice, not "the marketplace."

Then the writers of the Watchtower appendix say "correspondingly, the same argument could be used respecting the Greek word "Theos" - that's the word for God-without the article "ho" in John 1:1. If it doesn't have that article in front of it you can translate it "a god". And they go on to add, instead of translating John 1:1, "and word was deity," this grammar could have translated it, " and the word was a god". This runs more parallel with Xenothon's statement, "and the place was a market." You can see a parallel there.

When we take a look at the Dana and Mantey Manual Grammar of the Greek, we find the situation does mention these illustrations, but it mentions them somewhat differently. Here is the actual quote from page 148, 149 of their text:

> the article sometimes [*by the way, for those of you who are not into the technicalities of grammar, the word article refers to the word "the" - it's the definite article*] distinguishes the subject from the predicate in a copulative sentence.

In Xenothon's "Annabasis", the statement is made "and the place was a market." We have a parallel case there to what we have in John 1:1 and the word was deity. The article points out the subject in these examples. Neither was the place the only market, nor was the word all of God, as it would mean if the article were used with Theos.

What the Watchtower didn't quote in their appendix was the following statement: "As it stands, the other persons of the trinity maybe implied in the word Theos." Did you get that? You see, these two grammarians Dana and Mantey were full and total in their support of the doctrine of the Trinity, which would of necessity include the Deity of Jesus. Christ is one of the Persons of the Triune God and therefore God in His own right.

This Manual Grammar of the Greek Language wasn't designed to support the Watchtower's idea of "a god" in the tiniest degree. Professor Mantey sent to the Watchtower Society a letter on this subject in which he severely rebukes them for misquoting his Manual Grammar of the Greek Language.

The next example is from the revised edition of the Kingdom Interlinear Translation, produced in 1985. They have changed their appendix somewhat. In their revised edition of the KIT they have dropped all reference to Dana and Mantey, and they referred now to another source of authority, namely, the translator Phillip B. Harner. See page 1140 of this revised edition. They refer to his article entitled, "Qualitative Anarthrous Predicate Nouns". The KIT uses Harner's example of Mark 15:39 and also John 1:1 found in his article published in the Journal of Biblical Literature, Volume 92, in 1973. The KIT refers to page 85 of the article.

They say on this page, Phillip B. Harner said that such clauses as the one in John 1:1 with an Anarthrous predicate preceding the verb is primarily qualitative in meaning. They indicate that the Logos (that's the word for Jesus before He came to earth) has the nature Theos - the Greek word for God. There is no basis for regarding the predicate Theos as definite.

And on page 87 of his article, Harner concluded, "In John 1:1, I think that the qualitative force of the predicate is so prominent that the noun cannot be regarded as definite." Now, you say, okay, I'm not too technical myself. What does that mean? Basically what Harner is saying as an authority on Greek grammar, is that a noun that doesn't carry the article "the" in front of it can very often be viewed as an adjective instead of a noun. An adjective, of course, describes the quality of something. The noun is the person-the adjective describes the characteristic. So, therefore, Harner favored translating it ' the Word was Divine' or 'the Word was the same as God' or what God was, the Word was.

But you see, what the Watchtower people would not admit is that if any translator translates John 1:1 "the Word was Divine" then that translator is acknowledging that Jesus is God for the simple reason only God is Divine. Do you understand that? No creature is Divine. Divine is the word to describe the unique personal characteristics of the One True God. So, therefore, to call the Logos Divine is to say that the Logos is by nature the One True God. That's what the translators are really saying. The Watchtower people will not discuss that aspect of the word.

However, the situation is actually worse. When we take the article that's mentioned here in the appendix, "qualitative Anarthrous predicate nouns," we find out that these are some of the things that Phillip Harner really said in his article, and I'm just going to mention a few of them.

He mentions another translator by the name of Bruce Vawter. "Vawter explains the meaning of this clause in John 1:1 distinctly and lucidly-"the Word is Divine, but He is not all of Divinity for He (that's the Logos) has already been distinguished from another Divine Person". You see? In other words, Harner is supporting other Bible translators who agree with this use of the word "Divine" for Jesus.

Then Harner goes on, "In terms of the analysis that we have proposed, a recognition of the qualitative significance of Theos would remove some ambiguity in his interpretation by a differentiation between Theos as the nature that the Logos shared with God." Did you note that? You translate John 1:1 in a way that helps support the concept that the word Theos there brings out the idea that the Logos shares the nature of God. It says ho -Theos, the God, as the person to whom the Logos stood in relation.

Only when this distinction is clear can we say of the Logos that He was God. Harner says yes, if you make this distinction by using the word Divinity, then you clear the way for accepting that the Logos was God.

Perhaps the clause could be translated "the Word had the same nature of God." This would be one way of representing John's thought. "ho Logos" (that's "the Word") no less than ho Theos, the God, had the nature of Theos, God. Now I hope this is not too technical. It's establishing clearly that this translator, this expert on the Greek grammar, insists that you recognize that Jesus possesses the nature of God and can therefore be called God.

Finally, Harner does something very interesting. He lists five different ways in which John the Apostle could have written John1: 1, especially the last part of the verse, where the Watchtower translates "and the Word was a god." He has five different Greek statements to express that idea, and out of all five, only one of them could be translated, "the word was a god." We have Clause A, Clause B, Clause C, Clause D, and Clause E, and it's D that is expressed in a way that could be translated into English, "the word was a god." In Greek that is "ho Logos en Theos". That's the word order in the Greek that would allow a translator to satisfactorily translate into English John 1:1 "the word was a god." But that was not the way that John the Apostle wrote it. He wrote it on this list according to Clause B, "Theos en ho Logos."

So, therefore, Harner is bringing out very clearly and distinctly in his writing that whatever way you decide to translate John 1:1, the one way that you can't translate it is "the word was a god." So, you see, the Watchtower is again guilty of misquoting these outside authorities.

Here's another example I find interesting. This is based upon an article in the Watchtower-1st of January '63, page 95. This Watchtower article referred to a scholarly book written by Professor Ernest C. Colewell, entitled, "*What is The Best New Testament?*"

This book, published by the Chicago University Press, was first printed in 1952. In 1947, Professor Colewell made a study of a number of translations and put them to the test as to 64 citations in the Book of John. The Book contains what Professor Colewell considers the correct rendering of each of those 64 citations. The *New World Translation* was not released until 1950 so Professor Colewell could not include it in his list of tested translations. If any reader will look up what Professor Colewell has to say about these 64 citations, and will compare these to the *New World Translation*, he will see that the *New World Translation* merits a score of 64. This is the same perfect score which is given to Dr. Goodspeed's translation of the New Testament."

That sounds pretty good, doesn't it? The Society is claiming that the *New World Translation* scored the highest number of points according to Professor Colewell. They boldly claim their translation is right up there with the translation produced by Professor Goodspeed.

You know what they don't' mention. The basis for Colewell's rating system shows clearly the reasons for the *New World Translation*'s perfect score, although it is not a reliable translation. Professor Colewell's book compared various translations with 64 test points in the Gospel of John. Now note this - using the Greek text of Westcott and Hort as does the *New World Translation*, the perfect score actually applies to the Greek text of Westcott and Hort utilized by the *New World Translation* committee. It does not apply to the English translation that they produce from it. Isn't that incredible? They want to boast about it, and yet it has no bearing on their actual English translation at all. It was just that they picked a very good Greek text to make their English translation from. That's all it's showing-a most incredible state of affairs that they would want to boast about that.

Then we have the case of the Erdman's Handbook to the Bible. In the Watchtower of March the 15th, 1982, on page 23, the Society was publishing an article on their translation. It explains why Jehovah's Witnesses consider their translation the very best translation in the world. The Witnesses are thinking that the *New World Translation* is the world's best translation of the Holy Bible.

In the article in the Watchtower, the Society once again went to outside authorities to support their contention that their *New World Translation* was the best. One of the authorities they quoted was *Eerdmans Handbook to the Bible*. The Erdman's Handbook, which deals with, lists, and compares Bible translations, is accepted throughout the entire scholarly world as being an authoritative handbook. So to get your translation into that book with a favorable mention is definitely a feather in your cap.

This is what the Watchtower said about the Erdman's Handbook. "*The Eerdmans Handbook to the Bible* lists the *New World Translation* among the 14 main 20th century English translations." Therefore, it's up there amongst 10 of the 14 top translations into the English language. A friend of mine, David Reed, wrote to the publishers of that handbook, and drew this statement in the Watchtower to their attention, and he got this reply:

Dear Mr. Reed,

Thank you for your letter of 8th of October regarding the Erdman's Handbook to the Bible. We were staggered to discover that the Watchtower had used our inclusion of the *New World Translation* among our list of 20th Century English translations in support of its own cause. Our intention in including this translation on the list was to draw the reader's attention to the fact that this translation was one produced to support a particular viewpoint. Alongside the entry in the handbook, we said, "produced by the Jehovah's Witnesses emphasizing their interpretation of particular texts." This was meant to be a warning, not a commendation.

As soon as we were informed of the way the entry had been used by the Watchtower, we removed it from the list. Our updated list of main 20th Century English translations in the new revised edition of the *Eerdmans Hand-book to the Bible* now carries no mention of the *New World Translation*.

I enclose a photocopy of the revised script. Please feel free to quote from this letter in any way you feel would help to disabuse people who have been misled.

Yours sincerely,

Pat Alexander. Editorial Director

What do you think of that? It's incredible, isn't it, that they would use and misuse these outside authorities in such a blatant fashion to hoodwink Jehovah's Witnesses and other readers of the Watchtower literature into thinking that this is the best translation of the Bible that exists. In reality, it is among the worst.

Now we consider the letter from Julius R. Mantey. Professor Mantey wrote the Society in Brooklyn, New York, July the 11th, 1974, when it was brought to his attention how they were misusing his handbook in their index. He goes on to show them where they have misquoted him, and then he ends up with this example:

The above are only a few examples of Watchtower mistranslations and perversions of God's word. In view of the preceding facts, especially because you have been quoting me out of context, I hereby request you not to quote the Manual Grammar of the Greek New Testament again, which you have been doing for all these years. Also, that you not quote it or me in any of your publications from this time on."

Regretfully yours,

Julius R. Mantey

It took the Watchtower Society 11 years to remove that information out of their Bible. They finally, in 1985, produced the revised edition, and there for the first time, dropped all reference to Professor Mantey. It's a sad state of affairs, though, don't you agree, when people have to act in that way.

Here's a letter from Dr. William Barclay, one of the world's leading authorities on the Greek language. He's writing to Dr. Donald P. Schumaker of the Department of Bible Studies in Biola College.

> Dear Professor Schumaker,
>
> Thank you for your letter of August the 11th. The Watchtower article has, by judicious cutting, made me say the opposite of what I meant to say.
>
> What I was meaning to say, as you well know, is that Jesus is not the same as God in a certain sense. To put it more crudely, it is that He is of the same stuff as God. He is of the same being as God. The way the Watchtower has printed my stuff has simply left the conclusion that Jesus is not God, in a way that suits them.
>
> It was good of you to write, and I don't think I need to say anything more to make my position clear."
>
> With every good wish, yours sincerely,
>
> William Barclay

It's a sad state of affairs when a Bible translation committee has to stoop to that kind of tactic.

Let me give you a list of some of the mistranslations in the *New World Translation*. We will go first to John 1:1. We have already been talking about that quite a bit, but let's see what else we can bring out about it: John, Chapter 1, Verse 1:

> In the beginning was the Word, and the Word was with God, and the Word was a god.

I will list 15 quotations from articles and letters written by 15 of the leading scholars of the Greek language on this very subject of the Watchtower bible's translation of John 1:1. It's entitled, *"What Greek Scholars Really Think about the New World Translation's, 'The Word was a god.'"* Let me quote a few of these to you so you can get an idea of what real experts think.

Dr. Julius R. Mantey is the first one on the list. He says,

> It is a shocking mistranslation, obsolete and incorrect. It is neither scholarly nor reasonable to translate John 1:1, "the word was a god.

Dr. Bruce N. Metzger of Princeton, Professor of New Testament Language and Literature-he says about the *New World Translation,*

> A frightful mistranslation, erroneous and pernicious, reprehensible. If the Jehovah's Witnesses take this translation seriously, they are polytheists.

Dr. William Barclay of the University of Glasgow, Scotland-(we have just been referring to his letter):

> The deliberate distortion of truth by this sect is seen in their New Testament translation. John 1:1 was translated "the word was a god," a translation which is grammatically impossible. It is abundantly clear that a sect which can translate the New Testament like that is intellectually dishonest.

Do you understand this? Are you getting this loud and clear? Dr. F. F. Bruce of the University of Manchester, England-

> Much is made by Arian amateur grammarians of the omission of the definite article with the word God in the

phrase, "and the word was God." Such an omission is common with nouns in the predicative construction. The translation "a god" would be totally indefensible.

Now what is it? Are these world-renowned scholars deliberately telling lies? Or are they telling it like it is? If I'd been on that *New World Translation* committee and found after I had produced a Bible that was being criticized I would conduct an investigation. If leading scholars from around the entire world-the top men of Bible languages in the world today-were looking at my translation and going into print with remarks like that I would respond to their remarks vehemently. If I knew that I was right and I could prove it, what do you think I would do? I would sue those men for slander-that's what I would do-for denigrating my ability as a translator? But the Watchtower does nothing about it. They do nothing about it because they can do nothing about it, because what these men are saying is true.

By the way, just as a matter of interest, to help you to see and to show Jehovah's Witnesses the gross inconsistency in their way of translating John 1:1, make this as a cross-reference for yourself, Mark 12:26-27, and have the Witnesses look at both passages, John 1:1 and Mark 12:26 and 27 in their *Kingdom Interlinear* Bible. If you look at it very carefully yourself, you will discover that the expression in John 1:1 Theos En Ho Logos is exactly the same grammatical structure as the references to God in Mark, Chapter 12.

However, in Mark, Chapter 12, the Witnesses do not translate the word God as "a god." Neither do they translate it in lower case with a little "g." They translated it as God, capital "G" and with the definite article. Now why did they do that? Because they knew that that passage in Mark 12 was definitely referring to the Almighty God Himself. You see? So therefore they wouldn't translate it in any other way. This completely contradicts their method of translating!

They took the liberty of taking the same expression, the same construction in the Greek, and translating it as God. Study that a little bit and you will be able to use that with the Jehovah's Witnesses.

How about John 8:58? This is the debate that Jesus had with the Pharisees when they were getting real mad at Him, wanting to know who He thought He was, and finally challenging Him. They said, you're not greater than our father Abraham, are you? And Jesus really, really shook them. He said, "Abraham rejoiced to see my day, and he saw it and was glad." The Jews were utterly astounded that this mere man, this son of a carpenter from Nazareth could stand in front of them and say such a thing, because they knew that their ancestor Abraham had lived and died almost 2,000 years before this man Jesus was born. And yet Jesus stood there and said, 'hey listen, Abraham rejoiced to see my day and he saw it."

They said to Him, "you are not yet 50 years old and you've seen Abraham?" They just couldn't believe their ears. And then Jesus made it a thousand times worse in verse 58 by saying, "before Abraham was, I Am." And in doing so, He used the classic expression from the Old Testament, which was the unique identity of the Almighty God and Creator, the God of Israel when He had appeared to the people of Israel. He also said it through the prophet Isaiah (Is. 43:10) to the people. "that you must know that 'I Am.'" You see? And here is Jesus making that same statement. The words "I Am" by the way, imply the eternally existing God. It doesn't matter where you go in the stream of time to eternity past and to eternity future, God can always say "I Am- I exist." You see? So Jesus was claiming to be the Eternal God right there.

Well, you know, the Society just couldn't stand that. So naturally in their Bible they had to change it. The *New World Translation* reads in John 8:58:

> Jesus said to them most truly I say to you before Abraham came into existence, I have been.

Although this translation allows for the concept that Jesus existed in some form before Abraham, the Watchtower people would say, 'well, of course He existed in some form before Abraham because he was Michael the archangel up in heaven before he came to the earth, so that explains that okay.' But what they couldn't accept was the fact that Jesus didn't really just say 'I have been,' - He used that timeless and eternal expression of identity, "I Am."

If you look at the Greek there, the *Kingdom Interlinear*, on the left-hand side, you can see for yourself as plain as anything, it says "Ego Eimi"("I am"). So why did the Witnesses change it? In their footnote-they give their reason for doing it, and of course that footnote is nonsense. It doesn't explain a thing.

Incidentally, I thought you might be interested to learn a few points about that. I have various references to the different Bible translations, and the modified Bible translations that the Society has produced over the years and Watchtower articles, and I want you to notice the different ways in which they try to explain that situation in the footnote. Starting with the original *New World Translation* of 1950 (that was the first year their Bible ever came out) at John 8:58, "I have been" footnote. It says,

> after the Aorist infinitive clause, hence probably rendered in the perfect indefinite tense.

Perfect indefinite tense? There is no such animal as perfect indefinite tense. So they even got the tense wrong-they invented a tense. They found an imaginary tense.

Bible scholars patiently pointed that out to them, so when they brought out the Kingdom Interlinear Translation in 1969, the footnote reads a little bit differently. "I have been." It says "after the Aorist infinitive clause properly rendered in the perfect tense". See? The perfect tense, by the way, in the Greek language is a form of past tense. But the thing is that it isn't in the perfect tense, and it isn't in the perfect indefinite tense-it's a plain open and shut case of "I am" in the present tense. That's what it is. So the Society is speaking nonsense!

So then they went on to produce a large print translation of the Bible in 1974. In John 8:58 they had the footnote now "I have been, after the Aorist infinitive clause and hence, properly rendered in the perfect tense indicative." Okay?

And then finally, we have the Watchtower that goes back to February the 15th, 1957. It contains an article about Bible translations, which says,

> from the above, it is seen that the *New World Translation* is consistent with itself in rendering the historical present by rendering John 8:58 "I have been" instead of "I am.

Now we have got it down as the historical present. These people can't even make up their mind what the tense of the verb really is there at John 8:58. Ask any reliable grammarian, and he'll tell you that "I am" "Ego Eimi" is simply a statement in the present tense and nothing else.*

Therefore it is clear the Witnesses have hidden the deity of Christ by grossly mistranslating that particular verse.

Now I want to go to Colossians chapter 2, verse 9. This is speaking about Jesus, after His ascension back into heaven "because it is in Him that all the fullness of the divine quality dwells bodily." Some translations say "godhead" but they don't say divine quality.

When we look at the *Kingdom Interlinear* under the Greek section and the English words, it says, "in Him is dwelling down all the fullness of Godship bodily." Based on the Greek word, "theotetos"(godship). Godship means the state or condition of being God. Kingship means the state or condition of being king; rulership means the state or condition of being ruler; and Godship means the state or condition of being God. So what the writer of Colossians really

---

* footnote: In Biblical Greek all letters are in capitals. Translations into English are written with both upper-case and loxer-case letters.

said about Jesus is the condition of being God dwells fully, bodily in Christ. Again, it's a clear identification of His Deity, but the Watchtower has tried to water it all away.

Titus 2:13; most Bible translations state that as "our great God and Savior Jesus Christ", don't they? Isn't that what it says in Titus 2:13. Yes, our great God and Savior, Jesus Christ." And that's how the Greek should be translated into the English to be accurate. But now the problem with that is how does it identify Jesus? It doesn't just say our great Savior, does it? It says our Great God and Savior, Jesus Christ. That didn't suit the Watchtower, so they wrote, "while we wait for the happy hope and the glorious manifestation of the great God and of the Savior of us, Christ Jesus" there's a natural distinction in there. We're not waiting for one person or one thing-we're waiting for two. We're waiting for the manifestation it says of the great God (that's number one) and then also we're waiting for the manifestation of the Savior of us, Christ Jesus.

However, my friends, we should be able to see, even from a doctrinal point of view why that is a mistranslation, because who is it we're really waiting for? We're waiting for Jesus. We're waiting for His manifestation. Everybody knows that. And so, the Bible writers are telling us that that's what we're waiting for, and they are really saying we are waiting for the manifestation of our great God and Savior, Jesus-it's as simple as that. And it's ridiculous to modify the translation of the word of God in that way.

There is also a passage in 2 Peter, chapter 1, verse 1, which they have mistranslated once again in the same way. Again, you see at the end of that verse, the end of the greeting there, it says "of our God and Savior Jesus Christ." In their Bible, it says, "of our God and the savior, Jesus Christ. Check the Greek; it says nothing about "and the savior." Again, it's the kind of construction in the Greek language that should be translated into English "the God and Savior, Jesus Christ," or "our God and Savior, Jesus Christ."

Here's a little exercise you can do. You can compare that verse with 2 Peter chapter 1 with verse 11. There the construction is exactly the same, but instead of the expression "God and Savior" being used, the expression that Peter uses is "Lord and Savior." The wording is exactly the same. The grammatical structure of the sentence is also exactly the same. The only difference, instead of using the noun God, you're using the noun Lord. Not "God and Savior", but "Lord and Savior". Now note how they've translated that in their *New World Translation.*

> In fact, thus there will be richly supplied to you the entrance into the everlasting Kingdom of our Lord and Savior, Jesus Christ.

Funny, isn't it? They manage to get the translation right there, where they're using the word Lord and not God, but the same construction they can't get right because the word God is used. If this isn't playing games, I don't know what is. This is playing games with the word of God. We have to understand that makes the *New World Translation* a very bad mistranslation indeed.

We need to take a look at another very important point and that is the misuse of God's name in the Jehovah's Witnesses New Testament. Your Bible, if you're using the King James or the New American Standard or the NIV does not contain the Old Testament name of God anywhere in the New Testament - it's not there. But it is in the Watchtower New Testament in the *New World Translation.* They have their name, which they say is Jehovah, in their New World New Testament 237 times!

I am going to quote to you from their foreword, the introduction to their Bible, and listen to some of these remarks that they make about their approach to translation.

> Our primary desire has been to seek not the approval of men, but that of God by rendering the truth of His inspired word as purely and as consistently as our consecrated powers make possible. There's no benefit in self-deception. More than that, those who provide a transla-

tion for the spiritual instruction of others come under a
special responsibility as teachers before the Divine judge.
Hence, our appreciation of the need of carefulness.

Isn't that amazing? Incredible that they would say that
and then distort the translation of the Greek language.
It continues on page 10:

> Our endeavor all through has been to give as literal a
> translation as possible where the modern English idiom
> allows and where a literal rendition does not for any clum-
> siness hide the thought. That way, we can best meet the
> desire of those who are scrupulous for getting as near as
> possible, word for word, the exact statement of the origi-
> nal.

When you read this, you would think they were just
bending over backwards and moving mountains to make
sure they got it as exact as possible, wouldn't you? But that's
the last thing in the world they did on all those key verses
identifying Jesus.

The same thing applies to their use of the Divine name
from the Old Testament, bringing it forward and using it in
the New Testament. Now this is what they say about their
reason for putting Jehovah into the New Testament text.

> How is a modern translator to know or determine
> when to render the Greek words "kyrios" and "theos" into
> the divine name in his translation? By determining where
> the inspired Christian writers have quoted from the He-
> brew Scriptures and then he must refer back to the origi-
> nal to locate whether the Divine name appears there. This
> way he can determine the identity to give to "kyrios" and
> "theos" and he can clothe them with personality. Realiz-
> ing that this is the time and place for it, we have followed
> this course in rendering our version of the Christian Greek
> Scriptures; to avoid overstepping the bounds of the trans-
> lator into the field of exegesis, we have tried to be most
> cautious about rendering the Divine name, always care-
> fully considering the Hebrew Scriptures.

Did you note that? It's true, isn't it, that the writers of the New Testament did make many quotations from the Old Testament.

And it's also true that in the original documents of the Old Testament, the Divine name of God "Yahweh" did appear many times. So therefore, you would say well, okay, let's accept that. If a New Testament writer quotes from the Old Testament, and he's using a verse where the name is used, then I guess logically, he could bring it forward. But do you know how many quotations there are from the Old Testament part of the Bible that use verses where the Divine name is included? It is included fifty times. You know what that means don't you? That if the Watchtower people have used the name Jehovah in the New Testament 237 times, then 187 of those references have obviously got nothing to do with the Old Testament writings at all. Let me illustrate this for you.

In Acts, chapter 8, let's see where these wonderful experts, these scholars, stuck to that rule. Acts 8, starting in verse 22 - this is a conversation between the apostle Peter and Simon Magus, the magician. Simon had tried to buy the gifts of the Holy Spirit with money; and so Peter says to him, "Repent, therefore, of this baseness of yours and supplicate Jehovah."

Going on in verse 24, Simon said to Peter, "You men make supplications for me to Jehovah." Verse 25, "when they had given the witness thoroughly and spoken the word of Jehovah, they turned back to Jerusalem." Verse 26, "however Jehovah's angels spoke to Philip." You notice four times that name Jehovah is used there in this passage in Acts 8. Not one of those verses is a quotation from the Old Testament at all.

None of those verses has anything to do with anything that was written in the Old Testament. So they have broken their own rule, haven't they? And the truth of the matter is they broke the rule 187 times in order to smuggle that name into the New Testament text.

Now I think it's only fair to tell you that although the idea might seem logical to bring forward the divine name if it were in the Old Testament, it isn't necessarily true. Because you see is so happens that that Divine name in the Old Testament is really an Old Testament name for God, it is not a New Testament name. By the way, it's Yahweh not Jehovah. And Yahweh was His revelation of Himself to the people of Israel. It was for their benefit that he revealed himself as Yahweh, which means the eternal God of purpose. It is not a New Testament way of designating God at all. In the New Testament, God the Father is called God the Father. And the name that's given is Jesus Christ, as we just read, "our great God and Savior." Who? Jesus Christ. The name is Jesus Christ, but the separate identities are father and son-the father being identified simply as God the Father.

In the introduction to their Bible, they talk about the early manuscripts. I want to make a comment about this. All good translations of the Bible are based upon the oldest Greek documents available. Here's a list. The Sinaitic Manuscript. The Alexandria Manuscript. The Armenian Version. The Vatican Manuscript 1209 and so on. None of those early documents has the name Yahweh or Jehovah in the New Testament in any one place. So I would suggest that if the earliest documents available don't use the name, then we'd better not presume to insert it into our New Testament translations.

Chapter 3

The Gospel

So far we've been examining the Witnesses teachings with regard to prophecy and their special Bible, the *New World Translation.* We have seen where they have gone wrong. We have noted where they have misunderstood the meaning of key words in the Scriptures. We have considered the danger when verses are taken out of context. And more revealing, we have exposed the Watchtower's need to mistranslate and retranslate the Bible in order to try and support their wrong ideas.

Now we're dealing with the Jehovah's Witness gospel, and we're going to compare it with the true Gospel, which is outlined in the Holy Bible. Jehovah's Witnesses are very strong in their claims to be preachers of the gospel. They don't use that word, by the way, because to them it's a rather archaic and "religious" word. So, in their Bible it's translated as "good news". By the way, there's nothing wrong with that translation. Other modern translations will do the same thing because, in actual fact, that Old English word does mean good news.

They will draw your attention to Matthew 24:14, where the Gospel is referred to by Jesus. Matthew 24 is embedded in the great prophecy, which our Lord Himself gave to the disciples concerning His Second Coming, His Return and the End of the Age. Right in the center of His prophecy Jesus said in verse 14,

> And this good news of the Kingdom will be preached
> in all the inhabited earth for a witness to all the nations,
> and then the end will come.

The Jehovah's Witnesses will proudly tell you that it is their organization that alone is fulfilling that particular prophecy. They alone are the ones who are going out world-wide in all countries, taking from door to door the "good news" of the Kingdom. They're very proud of this effort!

Then they will turn you to the cover of The Watchtower, and they will point out that on the cover of The Watchtower it says, "Announcing Jehovah's Kingdom." And they will say that it's the major thrust of their work, to teach and to preach "the good news of the Kingdom."

Wait a minute. What are the ingredients of that gospel? The Jan. 15, 1980 edition of The Watchtower, which gives the title, Good Government-the Challenge, tells us that their gospel, their good news is concerning a government.

The Watchtower is entitled on page 9, "God's Government-Mankind's Only Hope." Now my friends, if you're familiar with the word of God and if you know the Gospel, you'll know that the Gospel presents the message of mankind's only hope, does it not? That's why it's such good news, because it's news of the only way that you can get right with God. But the Witnesses say that God's government is mankind's only hope, and that government is the center of their message.

When they come to your door and you say to them, what's your good news of the Kingdom all about? They'll immediately say something to this effect:

> The world is in desperate straits; the world is going from bad to worse, and if God were to leave us to our own devices, we would eventually destroy all of mankind from the face of the earth. But fortunately for us, Jehovah does not intend for that to happen. In fact, he has his government. It is a spiritual government, and it is composed of Jesus Christ and 144,000 footstep followers of Jesus who are going to constitute a spiritual government over mankind. And this spiritual government of Jesus and 144,000 is going to destroy all the existing governments of mankind, all the human governments. That spiritual government is going to take over the entire globe and all of earth's affairs. Jehovah's Witnesses who have been faithful to

God are going to be protected through that time of destruction of human governments. They're going to live
here on a paradise earth and they'll live under the rule of
that spiritual government of Jesus and the 144,000.

That's their message. It's a message about a government, which they claim is the main theme of the Bible. The
article goes on to say:

> And it is God's delight to provide humans with a good
> government...The magazine in your hands [they mean
> the Watchtower of course] has lived up to its title 'The
> Watchtower Announcing Jehovah's Kingdom.' Its pages
> regularly have emphasized the Kingdom message. Actu-
> ally God's government is the Bible's main theme.

Did you catch that? "God's government is the Bible's
main theme," say the writers of The Watchtower. Then they
go on to talk about the work of Jesus when He was on earth:

> After John baptized Jesus, God poured out his Holy
> Spirit to anoint Jesus as the One who would become king
> of the heavenly government ... A further revelation about
> this Government is that others from among humankind
> will have the privilege of reigning with Christ as king.
> Later, the apostle John wrote about those who will "rule
> as kings over the earth" along with Christ Jesus, giving
> their number as 144,000...Do you, however, appreciate
> the Bible's message? How would you answer if someone
> asked you, "What is the main theme of the Bible?"

Good question, isn't it? Now note their answer:

> Some years ago one of Jehovah's Witnesses, an elec-
> trician in a department store in Dayton, Ohio, had a fine
> opportunity to give an answer [to that question, "What is
> the main theme of the Bible?"] He was asked by the editor
> of the store's paper to write a review of the most enjoyable
> book he had recently read. He wrote, I will never finish
> reading this book in my lifetime. It begins by having a
> beautiful home destroyed by rebellion. Tragedy, disaster,

sorrow, murder and death follow. As the family multiplies, the plunge into darkness and despair accelerates. Centuries roll by, nations rise and fall, thousands of characters pass in review, every human emotion from stark raw hate to a martyr's love is encountered. Hope beginning as a faint spark grows to absolute assurance. A perfect government is to reestablish the beautiful home. Its ruler is the King, Christ Jesus; the government, the Kingdom of God; the family, the human race. The book is the Bible!

Interesting, isn't it? Did you notice there is not one word in that statement concerning the fact that Jesus died to pay the price for our sins? It does not mention that He rose from the dead that we might be declared righteous by God. Do you realize that? Not one word in this entire article deals with what the only hope of mankind is in Jesus Christ. The good news of the Kingdom as presented by Jehovah's Witnesses is a government.

So can you see how the entire thinking of Jehovah's Witnesses is centered in exclusively on this concept, a spiritual government composed of Jesus plus 144,000 other humans selected from the earth who are going to successfully rule over the earth? That is their idea of what the gospel really is for mankind.

What can we say about the Gospel from the Christian viewpoint and the Biblical standard? First of all we have to point out that there is only one Gospel in the Bible. Have you ever noticed that the definite article is used in front of the word Gospel? It's always called "the Gospel". In Romans 1:16, the apostle Paul says,

> "...I am not ashamed of the gospel, for it is the power of God for salvation to everyone who believes, to the Jew first and also to the Greek."

That's how the apostle placed the emphasis and the value and the power on the true Gospel of Holy Scripture. He said that Gospel is nothing to be ashamed of because it is the power of God for salvation to everyone who believes. Please notice though, he said "the Gospel." He didn't say "a gospel," or "one gospel among many gospels," he said "the Gospel or the good news."

Although there is one Gospel in the Holy Bible, it is given many titles. This is one of the areas in which the Jehovah's Witnesses have failed to understand the Word of God. This has caused great confusion in their thinking. So, I'm going to give you a list of verses under the idea of "one Gospel, many titles".

First of all Matthew 4:23, concerning the work of Jesus:

> ...Jesus was going about in all Galilee, teaching in their synagogues, and proclaiming the gospel of the Kingdom."

See that? No doubt about it. Our Lord, His Gospel, was definitely the "Gospel of the Kingdom."

Now, in Mark 1:1, which is the next Gospel account after Matthew, we'll notice a different title is given. It's,

> The beginning of the gospel of Jesus Christ, the Son of God.

That's interesting isn't it? Matthew called it the Gospel of the Kingdom; Mark called it the Gospel of Jesus Christ.

Let's move into the book of Acts and take a look at Acts 20:24. Paul is speaking about his own preaching activity, his own sharing of the Gospel with others. Acts 20:24:

> "But I do not consider my life of any account as dear to myself, in order that I may finish my course, and the ministry which I received from the Lord Jesus, to testify solemnly of the Gospel of the grace of God."

Do you see that? "The Gospel" not "a Gospel". There's only one Gospel. But here Paul definitely entitles it the Gospel of the grace of God.

Please turn to Romans 1:1:

> "Paul, a bond servant of Christ Jesus, called as an
> apostle, set apart for the Gospel of God."

So here's yet another descriptive term for the Gospel.
Now it is the 'Gospel of God'.

Okay, moving forward through the New Testament
letters, we'll stop at Ephesians 1:13. The apostle is reminding the Gentile converts to Christianity in Ephesus about
how Paul came and preached the Gospel to them. He re-
minds them about how they responded in faith to the Gospel and were saved. In discussing that in Ephesians 1:13,
he says,

> "In Him [that's in Jesus], you also, after listening to
> the message of Truth, the Gospel of your salvation-hav-
> ing also believed, you were sealed in Him with the Holy
> Spirit of promise..."

Now, Paul defines the Gospel as the "Gospel of salvation".

Finally, in the sixth chapter of Ephesians in the fif-
teenth verse, we see that yet another descriptive term is
used. Paul says to the Christians in verse 15,

> "And having shod your feet with the preparation of
> the "Gospel of peace."

So look at all those different ways of describing the
one and only Good News message, the one and only Gospel
of the Holy Bible.

Somebody might say, "Now wait a minute, surely
though they are different gospels, are they not?" The answer is "No they are not!" The Gospel of the Kingdom is the
Gospel of Jesus Christ is the Gospel of the grace of God is
the Gospel of salvation is the Gospel of peace. It is all of
those things, is it not? Of course it is all of these Divine
promises.

To round out our thinking, let's go back to Acts 28, and see what it says about Paul's preaching work there in verses 30-31.

> He [that's Paul] stayed two full years in his own rented quarters, and was welcoming all who came to him preaching the Kingdom of God and teaching concerning the Lord Jesus Christ with all openness unhindered.

Paul's preaching was the Kingdom... was Jesus... and was the Gospel. There's no question about that.

Let's enlarge a little bit on the subject. The Gospel writers and Matthew particularly, said that Jesus was going around preaching the Gospel of the Kingdom. Now, how did Jesus Himself do that? Let's take a look at Matthew 4 again. Please begin reading from Matthew 4:17. It says,

> From that time Jesus began to preach and say, 'Repent, for the Kingdom of heaven is at hand'.

Why did Jesus say, "...the Kingdom of heaven is at hand"? The answer is very simple. Because He Himself was the King of the Kingdom, and He was right there in their midst. He was standing there. Without Jesus there is no Kingdom.

It's all very well for the Jehovah's Witnesses to talk about this wonderful spiritual government made up of Jesus and 144,000. Let me tell you this, that without Jesus, there is no Kingdom of God, and there never will be without Him. And so, wherever Jesus is, there the Kingdom of God is. Wherever Jesus is, there the Kingdom is at hand.

According to Luke 17:20-21 on that subject, and we can see what our Lord says about the Kingdom. Verse 20:

> Now having been questioned by the Pharisees as to when the Kingdom of God was coming, He answered them and said, "The Kingdom of God is not coming with signs to be observed, nor will they say, 'Look, here it is!' or, 'There it is!' For behold, the Kingdom of God is in your midst."

Get the point? They were looking for the Kingdom in their day. They were looking for the full establishment of God's Kingdom. The Pharisees and the Jews believed according to Old Testament prophecy, that when the Messiah came with glory and power with His Kingdom then they would be taken out of bondage. They understood that they would be released from the yolk of the Roman Empire and become the leading nation of the world. They were very anxious for that to happen. When they questioned Jesus about these things, He said, in effect, "Forget it, for the Kingdom is not coming with signs to be observed. You won't say, 'Here it is!' or, 'There it is!' because the Kingdom of God is in your midst." He was really saying, "Listen, fellahs, I am the Kingdom. The kingdom's Me! And the kingdom's in your midst right now."

Jesus had a unique way of handling His preaching regarding "the Kingdom". His way of preaching the Gospel of the Kingdom was not to talk about future events. He did not talk specifically about a paradise earth. Jesus had very little to say about a paradise earth, and very little to say about people surviving the battle of Armageddon. Nor did He preach on living here on earth or being trained to live on a paradise earth. But He had an awful lot to say about Himself whenever He spoke about the Kingdom.

In Matthew 13, Jesus does something very interesting. He outlines a series of parables. Jehovah's Witnesses say that Jesus preaches the good news or the gospel of the Kingdom in all nations in these parables. Pleases notice the information that Jesus gives in these parables relating to the Kingdom. Beginning with Matthew 13:10-11:

> And the disciples came and said to Him, 'Why do You speak to them in parables?"

By the way, I think that I should mention a little point that perhaps you might not be aware of regarding the Biblical parables. Jesus did not spend His entire ministry speaking to people in parables. Preachers will say, "Jesus was the One who used parables to teach the people." The truth of the matter is that most of the time Jesus did not use parables. He spoke out very plainly and openly. If you look at the early chapters of Matthew's Gospel, you will find that Jesus came to the Jewish people as a Rabbi. They called Him Rabbi, and Rabbi He was, which is a teacher of the Law of Moses.

So, it's not surprising that in Matthew 5, 6, & 7, we find Jesus expounding on the Law of Moses. In very clear and definitive terms he explains to the Jews what the Law of God really meant, and doing so with the most immense authority imaginable. It really astounded the crowds because they had never heard such authoritative teaching before.

However, as time went by the people began to harden their hearts against Jesus. They began to reject Him as their Messiah. They began to refuse to accept Him as their King. They began to hate Him and despise Him. Then the time came when Jesus switched to the use of parables. And that is why the disciples came and spoke to Him about it, because they were surprised. In verse 10, they said to Him, "Why are you doing this? Why do You speak to them by the use of parables?" Now watch the answer very carefully in verse 11. "He answered and said to them, 'To you it has been granted to know the mysteries of the Kingdom of heaven...'" See the point? He's talking to the disciples about the Kingdom, but He tells them that it's a mysterious subject. He says, To you disciples it has been granted to know the mysteries of the Kingdom of heaven, but to them [that was to the rest of the Israelite people] it has not been granted.

Therefore [verse 13] I speak to them in parables; because while seeing they do not see, and while hearing they do not hear, nor do they understand. And in their case the prophecy of Isaiah 6 is being fulfilled, which says:

> You will keep on hearing, but will not understand;
> and you will keep on seeing, but will not perceive... [And

here's the reason why:] For the heart of this people has become dull, and with their ears they scarcely hear, and they have closed their eyes lest they should see with their eyes, and hear with their ears, and understand with their heart and return, and I should heal them.

So Jesus said, "They've hardened their hearts against Me; now I will speak to them in the mystery of parables." Afterwards, Matthew 13 goes on to explain how Jesus takes His disciples to one side and explains to them, and them only, the meaning of the parables. That's how it works.

In verses 3-9, Jesus speaks about the seed that falls on the four types of soil. In verses 24-30, He gives the parable of the wheat and the tares. In verses 31 and 32, He gives the parable of the mustard seed. In verse 33, Jesus uses the parable of the leavened bread. In verse 44, He uses the parable of the hidden treasure. In verses 45 and 46, He speaks of the parable of the pearl of great price. And in verses 47 and 48, He proclaims the parable of the dragnet.

All these parables, every one of them a mystery, and every one of them is relating to the Kingdom of God. Jesus is preaching the Gospel of the Kingdom. But when you analyze these parables, and when you allow the meaning of the parables to come right home to you, what do you discover? They're all parables that relate to Him and to people's relationship to Him, and to whether they are accepted by Jesus or to whether they are rejected by Him. That was His method of preaching the Gospel or the Good News of the Kingdom.

When Christ completed His ministry, He offered up His life on our behalf. He died and He rose again from the dead. He appeared to the disciples to prove the Resurrection, and then finally ascended back into heaven after giving final instructions to His disciples relating to the Kingdom. Then the disciples were ready to go forward into the world and preach the Gospel of the Holy Bible.

What did they preach about? Did they preach the message that Jehovah's Witnesses are bringing from door to door? Let's take a look at some of the examples we have in Scripture. The last two verses of Acts 28 are a description of the preaching work of Paul. It reads:H

> He stayed two full years in his own rented quarters, and was welcoming all who came to him, preaching the Kingdom of God, and teaching concerning the Lord Jesus Christ...

So that was the work of Paul in a nutshell. He was preaching the Kingdom of God and teaching concerning the Lord Jesus Christ, and that was the sum total of his Gospel. Nothing was preached about paradise earth. The disciples did not go into the world to teach about survival of Armageddon. Furthermore, the disciples did not preach about governments composed of 144,000 followers of Jesus.

Consider the beginning of the preaching work of the apostles in Acts 2 on the day of Pentecost. Let's see what the first great Gospel sermon was all about. Let's see if we can identify the key ingredients of the Gospel. Here the apostle Peter is speaking on the day of Pentecost. Acts 2 verse 14 says:

> But Peter, taking his stand with the eleven, raised his voice and declared to them: 'Men of Judea, and all you who live in Jerusalem, let this be known to you, and give heed to my words.'

Peter is now going to lay on these people the Gospel. In verses 22-24 we read:

> Men of Israel, listen to these words: Jesus the Nazarene, a Man attested to you by God with miracles and wonders and signs which God performed through Him in your midst, just as you yourselves know- this Man, delivered up by the predetermined plan and foreknowledge of God, you nailed to a cross by the hands of godless men and put Him to death. And God raised Him up again, putting an end to the agony of death, since it was impossible for Him to be held in its power.

The death and resurrection of Jesus Christ is the immediate and central thrust of the first Gospel ever given by the apostles of the church. See that? Then in the following verses, Peter uses the Old Testament and the prophecies of the Old Testament prophets to support his message. He finally says in verses 36-38,

> Therefore let all the house of Israel know for certain that God has made Him both Lord and Christ-this Jesus whom you crucified. Now when they heard this, they were pierced to the heart, and said to Peter and the rest of the apostles, 'Brethren, what shall we do?' and Peter said to them, 'Repent, and let each of you be baptized in the name of Jesus Christ for the forgiveness of your sins; and you shall receive the gift of the Holy Spirit. For the promise is for you and your children, and for all who are far off, as many as the Lord our God shall call to Himself.

And it was on that day as a result of that Gospel that 3,000 people received Christ and were converted to Christianity. Isn't that true? Now this is the real Gospel. This is the Gospel of the Holy Bible, and it always, without fail centers in on the Person and the work of our Lord Jesus Christ. Without that there is no Gospel. Without the redemptive work of Christ, nobody is going to get into that Kingdom, or the paradise earth! So the Gospel then, must center in on the Person and work of Jesus.

Now let's look at Acts 8, and consider verse 29 onwards. This concerns the case where Phillip the evangelist was sent to an Ethiopian official. The Ethiopian was sitting in his chariot and reading the scroll of the prophet Isaiah when the Spirit speaks to Philip:

> And the Spirit said to Philip, 'Go up and join this chariot.' And when Philip had run up, he heard him reading Isaiah the prophet, and said, 'Do you understand what you are reading?' And he [the Ethiopian] said, 'Well, how could I, unless someone guides me?' And he invited Philip to come up and sit with him. Now the passage of Scripture they were looking at was this [from the 53rd chapter

of Isaiah]... 'He was led as a sheep to slaughter; and as a lamb before its shearer is silent, so he does not open his mouth... the eunuch answered Philip and said, 'Please tell me, of whom does the prophet say this? Of himself, or of someone else?' And Philip opened his mouth, and beginning from this Scripture he preached Jesus to him.

You must understand something here, my dear friends. When verse 35 says that Philip preached Jesus to the Ethiopian, it meant that He started with this verse from Isaiah 53. What do you know about the 53rd chapter of Isaiah? It's the Gospel. It's all there in full detail, how Christ would pay the price for our sins, and would satisfy God and how God would raise Him from the dead. That's what Isaiah 53 is all about. Therefore, we'd better understand that this is the Gospel, and nothing else. The death of Jesus for our sins, His rising again from the dead in order that we might be declared righteous. The redemptive work of Christ is the Gospel.

Another passage where the Gospel is preached for the first time to a Gentile family can be found in Acts 10:34-38. Peter's in the house with with the family:

> And opening his mouth, Peter said: "I most certainly understand now that God is not one to show partiality".

He goes on to say, at verse 38:

> You know of Jesus of Nazareth, how God anointed Him with the Holy Spirit and with power and how He went about doing good and healing all who were oppressed by the devil; for God was with Him. And we are witnesses of all the things He did both in the land of the Jews and in Jerusalem. And they also put Him to death by hanging Him on a cross. God raised Him up on the third day, and granted that He should become visible, not to all the people, but to witnesses who were chosen beforehand by God, that is, to us, who ate and drank with Him after He arose

from the dead. Of Him all the prophets bear witness that
through His name everyone who believes in Him receives
forgiveness of sins.

That was the message that Cornelius and his family
heard and to which they responded in faith and were saved.
The Bible account goes on to tell that the Holy Spirit fell
upon them. That's the Gospel. This is the Gospel of the Holy
Bible. This is the Gospel of the apostles. How much more
testimony do we need?

Let's conclude the evidence with 1 Corinthians 15
where the apostle is recapitulating the Gospel once again
for the benefit of the Christians in Corinth. Those naughty
Corinthians who wouldn't behave themselves and had to be
reeducated all over again on all kinds of subjects and all
kinds of truths. In chapter 15 the apostle has to remind
them of the basic ingredients of the true Gospel. Beginning
in verse 1 he says:

> Now I make known to you, brethren, the gospel which
> I preached to you, which also you received, in which also
> you stand, by which also you are saved...

There it is. He is reminding them of the Gospel, which
he himself had preached which had resulted in their salvation.

Once again, the apostle is going to go over the simple
basic ingredients of the Gospel that he preached:

> For I delivered to you as of first importance what I
> also received [here it comes], that Christ died for our sins
> according the Scriptures, and that He was buried, and
> that He was raised on the third day according to the Scrip-
> tures, and that He appeared to Cephas, then to the twelve.
> (vv. 3-5)

That's the GOSPEL, my friends. And it doesn't matter
what name you put on it. You can call it the Gospel of God.
The Gospel of God's grace. The Gospel of Jesus Christ. The
Gospel of peace. The Gospel of salvation, or the Gospel of

the Kingdom. That is the only Gospel there is in the Holy Word of God. Are you with me? Yes, that's the only Gospel that there is, and it's the only Gospel that there ever will be. If Jesus Christ does not stand at the very heart of any Gospel message, then it is not the true Gospel of the Holy Bible.

I don't care who it is that comes to your door or who you meet at the local market or who wants to preach to you on campus at college or whatever it is; If they dare to start talking about what they think the Gospel is, and they don't tell you how Jesus died for your sins and rose again from the dead that you might declared righteous, then they are not giving you the Gospel of the word of God.

The Resurrection is an essential element of the Gospel. Don't forget my dear friends, in your own sharing of the Gospel that the Resurrection of Christ is just as an essential ingredient of the Gospel as His death. Look, at 1st Corinthians 15, verse 14:

> and if Christ has not been raised, then our preaching
> is vain, your faith also is vain.

Again in verse 17:

> and if Christ has not been raised, your faith is worth-
> less; your are still in your sins.

Look at this carefully. The Gospel is not just that Jesus died for you; the Gospel is that Jesus died for you and rose again from the dead in order for God to declare you righteous. It is very important to understand the real ingredients of the Gospel.

Now on the face of that, what could we honestly say about the preaching of Jehovah's Witnesses from door to door and their claim to be fulfilling Matthew 24:14, "...the good news [the gospel] of the Kingdom will be preached in all the world for a witness to all the nations, and then the end will come." Are they preaching the Gospel? No, I'm afraid not.

Therefore, I have to take this opportunity to issue a warning to Jehovah's Witnesses and to all others like them that would dare to bring a false gospel to the people. I'm going to start with a passage of Scripture in 2 Corinthians 4 verse 3 which talks about the Gospel that the apostles preached to the people.

> And even if our Gospel is veiled, it is veiled to those who are perishing, in whose case the god of this world has blinded the minds of the unbelieving, that they might not see the Light of the Gospel of the glory of Christ, who is the image of God. For we do not preach ourselves but Christ Jesus as Lord, and ourselves as your bondservants for Jesus' sake. For God, who said, 'Light shall shine out of darkness,' is the One who has shone in our hearts to give the Light of the knowledge of the glory of God in the face of Christ. (vv. 3-6)

Here we've once again got the Gospel. I want you notice certain tremendously important things that the apostle has to say about the true Gospel. He says that if it is veiled, it is veiled to those who are doomed. It is veiled to those who are perishing. What is a veil? All the ladies know what a veil is. The women in the Middle East to this very day wear a veil. It conceals their faces. It's part of their Moslem heritage to do that, and it conceals the face so that you cannot see it. So if Paul says that our Gospel, that's the Gospel preached by the apostles, if it's veiled so you can't see it, it's veiled to those who are perishing. And it says that Satan has a hand in this. Verse 4, "in whose case the god of this world [obviously Satan] has blinded the minds of the unbelieving..." Please notice. It doesn't say in that verse that Satan has blinded the *eyes* of the unbelieving. They can see and they can read, and for that matter, they can hear. But Satan has blinded their *minds* so that something doesn't penetrate.

What is it that Satan veiled? What it is that he's trying to blind people's minds about. What it is that he does not want to penetrate through at any price? The rest of the verse says, "that they might not see [now here it comes] the light of the gospel of the glory of Christ, who is the image of God." Satan doesn't care a fig what else they see. He doesn't care two pennyworth of lukewarm cheesecake (if you'll pardon the expression) whether somebody spends the next 100 years describing the paradise earth. He doesn't care. In fact, he'd probably laugh. He doesn't care if somebody sits down and spends the next 100 years explaining the 10 Commandments to them. He will probably think that's very funny. But what he doesn't want them at any price to see and understand and respond in faith to is "the gospel of the glory of Christ, who is the image of God." Get the point?

Paul emphasizes it in verse 5. "For we do not preach ourselves but Christ Jesus as Lord..." And then in verse 6, "For God, who said, 'Light shall shine out of darkness,' is the One who has shone in our hearts [that's the hearts of the believer, the ones that have got the message]" And what's the message we've got? "To give the light of the knowledge of the glory of God in the face of Christ."

There is nothing about a paradise earth anywhere in that message. There is nothing about a spiritual government of 144,000. It just isn't there! The Holy Bible is saying that it doesn't matter how glorious God's plans are for the future, or how wonderful He's going to make this earth. It doesn't matter a row of beans if you're not going to be there. You're not going to be there unless you hear the Gospel of Jesus Christ and understand that Gospel, and respond in faith to the Gospel, and get saved.

Therefore, I would end this message, continuing the warning to the Watchtower Society by drawing them to Galatians 1:6. Paul had been privileged to preach the true Gospel of the Bible, the Gospel about Jesus to the Galatians. Many of them had responded and received Christ and become Christians. And yet some people had come out from Jerusalem. We call them Judaizers; they were people claiming to be Christian. In reality they were Jews who secretly wanted to convert the Gentiles back to the Jewish religion and get them to circumcise themselves and undertake the law of Moses in order to get saved. Paul is just about ready to crush these people because of their heresy. And so he says to the Galatians about these Judaizers in verses 6 and 7:

> I am amazed that you are so quickly deserting Him who called you by the grace of Christ, for a different gospel; which is really not another; only there are some who are disturbing you, and what they really want to do is to distort the Gospel of Christ.

They're trying to distort the true Gospel; they're trying to replace the real, genuine Gospel with a perverted edition of the Gospel. Now look at the warning in verse 8:

> But even though we, or an angel from heaven, should preach to you a gospel contrary to that which we have preached to you, let him be accursed.

Let me tell you my friends, about that word translated "accursed" in English. In the Greek the word is anathematize. To anathematize is the very furthest degree a curse can go. If God anathematizes a person, then it's good bye forever. The destiny of that one who has been anathematized by God can be no other place than the lake of fire or Gehenna for all eternity.

So important was this to the apostle that he repeats himself in verse 9:

> As we have said before, so I say again contrary to that which you received, let him be accursed [anathematized].

That's how serious the situation is. The apostle, divinely directed, writing words God-breathed, speaking not his own thoughts but the thoughts of the Holy Spirit, has uttered the decree of the anathematizing of those who deliberately bring a false gospel to the people. Now can you understand how serious the position of Jehovah's Witnesses is?

You could hear their gospel a thousand times and it would never save you. Why? Their gospel is a counterfeit from top to bottom. The key ingredients of the true Gospel, namely, that Jesus died to pay the price for your sins and rose again from the dead that you might be declared righteous are totally missing from this gospel of the Kingdom preached by Jehovah's Witnesses. It's up to us as Christians to help the Witnesses see the seriousness of their position.

Chapter 4

The Return of Christ

We must be extremely careful when approaching the Word of God! If we manage to arrive at a false conception of any one of the fundamental teachings of the Bible, and then it will follow as night follows day, we will misunderstand other fundamental teachings. You see, all the fundamental truths of the Bible are all linked together. Therefore, if you get one out of perspective, it causes you to push the other doctrines out of perspective as well.

In this case, the Society's understanding of how Jesus is to return is linked with their understanding of the resurrection of Christ. The Witnesses are taught that when Jesus died and his body was placed in the tomb, that physical human body never emerged from the tomb again.

The Witnesses explain the absence of the body from the tomb by saying that God must have dissolved it completely away into gases or dissolved it into nothing. So what rose out of the tomb when Christ was resurrected was purely spirit. Jesus rose as a spirit from the dead. He ascended back into heaven as a spirit, and that's what enabled Him to become Michael, the Archangel again.

The Bible says in Hebrews, Chapter 1, that angels are spirits. And also because they are spirits, they are invisible. It is this concept of the invisibility of spirit life that guides the Jehovah's Witnesses in their understanding of how Christ returns.

Let's look at a reference to a Watchtower textbook called *You Can Live Forever in Paradise on Earth*. This is a quotation from the book that will assist you in understanding how the Jehovah's Witnesses understand the return of Christ. On page 146 the subheading reads, "Does Christ Come Back to Earth?" It says:

> To return does not always mean that one goes to a literal place; thus, sick persons are said to return to health, and a former ruler or king may be said to return to power.

> In a similar way, God told Abraham, 'I shall return to you next year at this time and Sarah will have a son.' Jehovah's return meant not literally returning, but returning his attention to Sarah to do what He had promised.

The Witnesses go on to say,

> In the same way Christ's return does not mean that He literally comes back to this earth. Rather, it means that He takes Kingdom power towards this earth and turns His attention to it. He does not need to leave his heavenly throne and actually come down to earth to do this.

The Watchtower teaches that in 1914 God's time arrived for Christ to return and to begin ruling. In addition they profess,

> Jesus doesn't really have to come back. He doesn't have to come back in any literal sense. He's up there in heaven at the right hand of the Father, Jehovah. And in God's due time, Christ can turn His "attention" to the earth and begin influencing Earth's affairs and taking over the rulership of the earth from His position in Heaven. He doesn't have to return.

I submit to you that such a concept is in reality a total denial of the real truth of what the Bible is teaching, that Jesus is going to come back in a very literal way. We are looking for Him to come back. This is the great hope of the Church, is it not? Jesus will literally Himself return as the Scriptures say.

I'm reminded at this juncture of 1 Thessalonians Chapter 4, which even in the Watchtower Bible, speaks in very precise and emphatic terms of the return of our Lord. Starting with Verse 16,

> Because the Lord Himself will descend from heaven with a commanding call, with an archangel's voice, with God's trumpet, and those who are dead in union with Christ will rise first. Afterward, we the living who are surviving will together with them be called away in the clouds to meet the Lord in the air, and thus, we shall always be with the Lord.

That's their Watchtower Bible. That's clear enough, isn't it? "The Lord Himself will descend from Heaven." That doesn't sound like Jesus staying up there, does it, and just turning His attention to the earth? It says also that the Church will be called away to meet the Lord where? "In the clouds."

We don't think in terms of air, which is part of our atmosphere, as being an ingredient of heaven, do we? It's obvious that the Bible is describing Christ returning to the scene of this earth in a very literal sense.

So why does the Watchtower take this position? It all stems from the fact that they falsely predicted the return of Christ originally for the year 1874. When Charles Russell began his Bible study group in 1870, he and his young friends (young people in their late teens and early twenties) were making their initial study of the Bible. They were very interested in Bible prophecy and Bible chronology. They very quickly got the idea of trying to calculate the time of the Lord's return.

It didn't take them long to come up with the date of 1874. They used similar calculations to those used by William Miller who had preached to the Adventists and had calculated that the Lord would return in the year 1844. When the prophecy failed, of course, it was a great disappointment among the Adventists. They tried various ways to get around the problem. Charles Russell as well used the same type of calculations and moved it all forward a certain number of years and projected it for 1874.

Of course when 1874 came, there was no visible, literal return of Jesus, which is what they were expecting. So Russell hit on the idea of rather than giving up that date and admitting that he was wrong, he came up with this wonderful idea. Jesus had definitely come back in 1874 and that their calculation was absolutely right. He hadn't come back physically and visibly-he had come back *spiritually* and *invisibly*. So he was able to maintain that fiction, that figment of imagination, and he persuaded all his followers that yes, this is what had really happened - Christ had returned invisibly in 1874.

For forty solid years, the early Witnesses of those days (the followers of Russell) went around telling everyone that Jesus had already returned. When people said, "Well, we can't see Him," then they would say, "Ah, yes, because you see He did not return literally and physically, but in a spiritual sense invisibly, and you can only see Him if you have the eye of faith." Isn't that amazing? But that's what they were teaching.

They have found some verses in the Bible, though, that they think support them in this idea of Jesus not returning visibly or physically. The first one they use is in John 14, verse 19.

> After a little while, the world will behold me no more, but you will behold me, because I live and you shall live also.

Actually He was talking about His coming death and then His resurrection. When Jesus died and His body was laid in the tomb, it's true that the world of that time - the world of unbelieving mankind- did not see Jesus. When He rose from the dead, although He rose literally and physically, He appeared only to His own disciples, they were the ones who saw Him.

But the Witnesses take that verse when He says, "In a little while the world will behold me no more" and they try and extend it down through all generations of mankind. Jesus was obviously talking about the world of his day. It's true that the world at that time, or the generation of that time, with the exception of the disciples, did not see Jesus again. That is simply the thought behind the statement.

They also like to use Hebrews 10:10 which says:

> By this will we have been sanctified through the offering of the body of Jesus Christ once for all.

In the *New World Translation*, it adds a word. It says, "the offering of the body of Jesus Christ once for all *time*." And on the basis of that addition, the Watchtower leaders interpret it to mean that Jesus has offered His human body as a sacrifice forever; therefore, He cannot take it back. If He didn't take it back, then He must have risen as a spirit and, therefore, He can return invisibly. You see the chain of thinking behind that? This then becomes a basis for one of their reasons for saying that Christ would not return visibly because He would not have a literal, physical body to return in.

What does that Scripture really mean? Well, if we couple it with Hebrews Chapter 7 and take a look at a few verses there, the meaning becomes very clear.

Starting in verse 24 of Hebrews 7 which is talking about Jesus, "He, on the other hand, because He abides forever, holds His priesthood permanently." Verse 25,

> Hence, also He is able to save forever those who draw near to God through Him since He always lives to make intercession for them, for it was fitting that we should have such a High Priest, holy, innocent, undefiled, separated from sinners, exalted above the heavens, who does not need daily like those high priests to offer up sacrifices first for His own sins and then for the sins of the people, because this He did once for all when He offered up Himself. (vv. 25-27)

In other words, this once-for-all sacrifice of the body of Jesus was in contrast with the repeated, never-ending year-by-year sacrifices that the priest of Israel had to offer, because those sacrifices in reality were not effective. They were only symbolic, but the sacrifice of Jesus, because it was totally effective, did not have to be repeated. It was a one-time offering.

But that has nothing to do with whether or not He can be raised physically from the dead. That only has to do with the value of His sacrifice.

Here's another Watchtower argument. If Christ remained a man and retained His physical human body and nature, then He would be lower than the angels. And for that, they take you to Hebrews, chapter 2, verse 7. There the Scripture is talking to man, and the writer here is applying it to Jesus.

> But one has testified somewhere saying, what is man thou rememberest Him? Or the son of man that thou art concerned about Him? Thou has made Him for a little while lower than the angels...

(Hebrews 2:6-7)

It's true that man in his present condition is lower than the angels.

The angels, at the moment, are a higher order of life than man. They have greater power then man; they have greater intelligence than man. But it says in the Scripture, "thou has made Him for a little while lower than the angels."

In fact, the truth of the matter is that the destiny for Jesus, even though He became a man of flesh and blood like us for awhile, was to have His physical body and human nature taken by God. He would also be raised from the dead, and glorified. He would be raised to a position way above the angels. And it's also the privilege of the Body of Christ, the true Christians, to share that same inheritance with

Jesus. We will be changed in that way. Even though we at the moment are lower than the angels, we will ultimately be much higher than the angels.

That's why in 1 Corinthians chapter 6 in verse 3 you will see that we are eventually going to be in the position to judge angels. It says in verse 3, "Do you not know that we shall judge angels? How much more matters of this life?" That's ultimately going to be our position when we're glorified with Christ.

Now remembering that our bodies are to be changed in the same way that Jesus' body was changed. 1 Corinthians 15, verses 42 and 43 lists the great changes to take place. It says "in the resurrection of the dead, it is sown a perishable body, and it is raised an imperishable one. The body is sown in dishonor, but it is raised in glory. It is sown in weakness, but it is raised in power."

My friends, when you have a body, which has become immortal and a glorified nature to go with it, then you will be higher than angels, even though you are still essentially human. This is an important truth that the Jehovah's Witnesses have entirely failed to understand.

The Witnesses have another verse in 1 Corinthians Chapter 15, verse 50. "Now I say this, brethren, that flesh and blood cannot inherit the Kingdom of God, nor does the perishable inherit the imperishable." On the basis of that verse they say, "Hey, listen, it's quite clear that flesh and blood cannot inherit the heavenly Kingdom. That cannot be done."

Well, of course, Christians agree with them. Flesh and blood cannot inherit the heavenly Kingdom, but when Christ was raised physically from the dead, was He flesh and blood? No. He certainly was not.

In Luke, chapter 24, Jesus Himself very carefully makes that distinction when He is asserting his physical nature and denying that He is just a spirit. Look at Luke chapter 24, verse 36:

> While the disciples were talking, He himself stood in
> their midst. They were startled and frightened and
> thought that they were seeing a spirit.

Notice that? The Jehovah's Witnesses believe that
Jesus was raised a spirit. Now, the Bible tells us that mo-
mentarily the disciples thought that they were seeing a
spirit, but Jesus soon corrects them in verse 38. He says,
"Why are you troubled, why do doubts arise in your hearts?
See my hands and my feet" (hands and feet are physical
things) "that it is I myself. Touch me and see, for a spirit
does not have [what?] flesh and bones." Please notice. Jesus
is describing his resurrection body, and He very carefully
and very accurately avoids using the expression "flesh and
blood." He is not flesh and blood anymore.

The natural body-the normal life cycle for everyone
living on this earth under present conditions, from the time
of Adam on down-has been what we called the "flesh and
blood" life cycle. And that is the natural body-the natural
man.

But the resurrection body does not depend upon a
bloodstream. The resurrection body is sustained by the
power of the Holy Sprit within. (See Romans 8:11) The Spirit
of God is what imparts directly, life to the physical body.

Now in that condition, we can inherit the Kingdom of
God. We cannot inherit the Kingdom of God as flesh and
blood, but we can inherit the Kingdom of God as flesh and
bones with our glorified bodies. This is another important
truth that the Jehovah's Witnesses have entirely failed to
realize.

So because of this, their false reasoning-Jesus cannot
have a human body; therefore, He can become invisible and
He can come back as a spirit invisibly. On the basis of that,
they are still teaching this concept. In fact, now they teach
that Jesus came back in 1914 in that invisible spirit condition.

All their authority is based on this false premise of
Christ's return. By the way-the invisible return of Christ in

1914 began the final generation of mankind. According to the Witnesses, this includes the fulfillment of all the prophecies in Matthew 24. All the signs of the times and the things to happen during the last generation have happened or will happen for this 1914 generation. In verses 45 through 47 of Matthew 24, Jesus declares that there will be a faithful slave whom He would appoint over all His belongings. The Jehovah's Witness leaders say, "yes, we are that faithful slave. Jesus came back in 1914 and shortly thereafter, he appointed us to be the slave to represent Him in the entire world in fulfillment of that Matthew 24 prophesy."

You see how distorted their thinking gets on the basis of one false doctrine about the resurrection leading into another false doctrine about the return of Christ?

Now of course the question is, do the Scriptures in the Bible talk about the coming of Jesus in a literal, physical way? We've already looked at one in 1 Thessalonians chapter 4 which says, "the Lord Himself will descend from heaven, and we will be called away to meet Him in the air." That would be one good verse.

A lot of people quote Revelation, chapter 1, and verse 7. Let's take a look at that. It's a very well known passage of Scripture. It says,

> Behold, He is coming with the clouds and every eye will see Him, even those who pierced Him, and all the tribes of the earth will mourn over Him even so, Amen.

That sounds pretty clear, doesn't it? But the Jehovah's Witnesses will say, "no! It does say, that every eye will see Him, but they're not going to see Jesus literally. They will "see" Him through the conditions that are taking place on the earth." In other words, all the terrible things that are going to go on during the Tribulation will prove to the various tribes of the earth that the invisible Jesus is indeed manifesting His power.

Now, I think that's a gross distortion of Scripture. It just simply says what it means, and it means what it says. But the question is, how do you prove that to a Jehovah's Witness who has such a prejudiced viewpoint?

I don't use that particular verse myself, to be frank with you. But I'll tell you the ones I do use. I start with Matthew 24, verse 30. Beginning in verse 29:

> Immediately after the Tribulation of those days, the sun will be darkened, and the moon will not give its light. The stars will fall from the sky, and the powers of the heaven will be shaken.

That seems to me to be clearly talking about a period in world history immediately coming at the end of the Tribulation period. And if you are students of the Bible, you probably believe, as I do, that's a seven-year period of time culminating with the Battle of Armageddon and the return of Christ, with the exception of Christians who hold the "Preterist" view of prophecy.

The Scripture says immediately after the Tribulation; "The sun's going to be darkened and the moon will not give it's light". In other words, the whole atmosphere is going to be in a state of darkness and gloom. And it's in that condition that verse 30 becomes fulfilled.

> Then the sign of the Son of Man will appear in the sky and all the tribes of the earth will mourn and they will see the Son of Man coming on the clouds of the sky with power and great glory.

Can you see how dramatic that is? If we can visualize that because of the enormous cataclysm of the Tribulation and the Battle of Armageddon, there is so much debris and stuff in the atmosphere that even the light of the sun has been cut off, and the reflected light of the moon isn't shining anymore. And the earth is in a darkened condition; and then suddenly, in an enormous blaze of glory, the Son of Man is seen coming on the clouds of the heavens. This will be a tremendous and awe-inspiring moment for mankind.

It's obviously so spectacular that everybody is going to see it. Now, the Witnesses use some very weird arguments against this. They will say, "Well, wait a minute, if Jesus comes down to Palestine to Jerusalem, how are the people around on the other side of the planet going to see Him?" What nonsense! Jesus only has to take 24 hours to slowly descend from His position right out there in space, and the entire globe will have turned on its axis, so everybody will have had an opportunity to see this glorious manifestation of Christ returning towards the surface of the earth.

Matthew 24:30 says, "all the tribes will see the Son of Man." However, the Society says they are going to see, not literally, Jesus, but they're going to see the destruction going on all around them, and that's going to mentally convince them that Christ is taking over. That's the Society's interpretation.

But in verse 30, it doesn't say that they will see the "sign" of the Son of Man. It says they will see the "Son of Man". And regarding the title, the "Son of Man", what does that mean? He is a man. Yes, His title as "Son of God" is an identity to show his Godship, and His title, "Son of Man", is to show His humanity and His human condition. So it's the human Son of man they see coming on the clouds of the sky with power and great glory.

We need to take a look now at the meaning of the Greek word, "parousia" and the Watchtower interpretation of "parousia". Page 340, of the Watchtower book, *Reasoning from the Scriptures* - this is what is says under the return of Christ in this little book. It says,

> Definition-before leaving the earth, Jesus Christ promised to return. Thrilling events in connection with God's

Kingdom are associated with that promise. It should be noted, however, that there is a difference between coming and presence.

Now you might ask, what's that got to do with anything?

The Society's leaders discovered that there were a number of different Greek words in the Bible that were used by the Bible writers to talk about the "return" of Jesus. One of them "erchomai" is normally translated "coming," and then the other "parousia" is sometimes translated coming and is sometimes translated presence.

So the Watchtower book goes on to say,

> Thus while a person's coming associated with his arrival or return occurs at a given time, his presence may thereafter extend over a period of years. In the Bible, the Greek word, "erchomai" meaning to come, is also used with reference to Jesus directing His attention to an important task at a specific time during His presence.

Well, that's nonsense. That's just Watchtower gobbledy-gook and double-talk. You cannot be present until first you've come, isn't that true? Or am I not making sense? You've got to come to a specific meeting place, i.e. a certain church, before you can be present in that church. Isn't that true?

The Witnesses are trying to convey the idea that Jesus can be present with us without actually coming. You have to realize that what we're dealing with here is a strange setup as far as the Witnesses' teaching is concerned.

In *Vine's Expository Dictionary* the word "coming" has a number of Greek words, not just one or two, but quite a number, that can be translated "coming". This is what Vine's says about "parousia". "Literally a presence, 'para', with being and denoting as both an arrival and a consequent presence with." The word parousia, therefore, "ousia" denotes both an arrival and a consequent presence with.

For instance, in a papyrus letter (this is a non-Biblical letter) written in the early Greek language, a lady speaks of the necessity of her parousia in a place in order to attend to matters relating to her property there. In other words, this lady was talking about coming to a particular place and being present there for awhile in order to conduct her affairs.

Paul speaks of his parousia in Philippi, Philippians 2, verse 12, in contrast with his "apousia", his absence.

Parousia is used to describe the presence of Christ with His disciples on the Mount of Transfiguration. When used of the return of Christ at the Rapture of the Church, it signifies not only His momentary coming with His saints, but His presence with them from that moment until His revelation and manifestation to the world.

In some passages, the word gives prominence to the beginning of the period, the course of the period, or to the conclusion of the period. So we can see that obviously the Greek word "parousia" can be used in a number of ways - coming or arrival, and being present with us, of course, would be two examples of that.

But the Society has tried to tie themselves down to just one interpretation of that Greek word. So in their Bible, whenever the word parousia is used, they translate it into the English as "presence." Hence, they can support the contention that Jesus is already present, although He hasn't come.

Furthermore, they claim that "parousia" denotes an "invisible presence." But in the Bible, we have two examples of a "visible" parousia. We have 2 Corinthians, chapter 7, and verses 6 and 7. Paul is talking about Titus, how when Paul was in Macedonia, Titus came to visit him and spend some time with him. We read in verse 6, "But God who comforts the depressed, comforted us by the coming of Titus." Does your Bible say coming there? Then in verse 7 we read, "and not only by his coming, but also by the comfort with which he was comforted in you..."

It is clear that the Scripture is talking about the literal, physical coming of somebody-not an invisible spiritual return, because Titus was very much a human, wasn't he? Titus was not an invisible spirit.

Then in Philippians, chapter 1, we have the same usage of the word there, to denote a literal, visible physical presence. Philippians 1, verse 26 Paul is talking to the Philippian Christians himself. He says, "so that your proud confidence in me may abound in Christ Jesus through my coming to you again." The word is parousia, and so the Watchtower Bible translates it "through my being present with you" again. But either way, coming or presence, it's a literal, physical presence that we're talking about in the case of Paul. He's literally going to the Philippian church and being with those Christians there.

A final verse, which really to my mind nails the whole problem, is in Hebrews 9:28.

> So Christ also having been offered once to bear the sins of many [that happened when He came the first time] shall appear a second time for salvation without reference to sin to those who eagerly wait for Him.

Now do you see that word, "appear?" To say something about somebody appearing a second time argues that they've already appeared a first time. Isn't that true? Well, when Jesus appeared the first time, did He come in an invisible, spiritual presence? No. He came literally and physically. People could see Him, and they could get hold of Him and feel Him, and they could listen to Him, because His presence with them the first time was a literal, physical, visible presence.

So when it says, "when He appears a second time" it literally again implies a visible, literal, physical presence of Christ. It's interesting if you make the Witnesses look at their *Kingdom Interlinear Translation*, under verse 28; it says, "the Christ was offered once for all time to bear the sins of many, and the second time that He appears, it will be apart from sin," Under the Greek word, it says, "He will be made visible." Did you catch that? That's the meaning of that Greek word. There's no question about it. The Bible teaches abundantly the literal, physical, visible return of our Lord at the End of the Age to usher in His Kingdom and to bring an end to the Tribulation period.

Finally, in 1 Corinthians 11:26 we read about communion. Paul is teaching the early Christians about partaking of the bread and the wine. The Apostle is saying something very important about this regular ritual or ordinance that's carried out in the church. In fact, we're still carrying it out to this very day. Jehovah's Witnesses do it as well. They only do it once a year on the anniversary of the Jewish Passover. Verse 26 reads: "For as often as you eat this bread and drink the cup, you proclaim the Lord's death until He comes." See the point?

The Witnesses have been claiming all along, that Jesus has already come, He returned invisibly in 1874. Then they changed their teaching and claimed that He returned and took over His Kingdom invisibly in 1914. And so if the rule is that by partaking of the bread and wine, you proclaim His death until He comes, what on earth are they still partaking for? It's redundant. Jesus has already returned according to their Biblical interpretation. He's already done every bit of returning that He's ever going to do.

And yet here they are, mechanically, every year, the anointed class among them, getting together in their Kingdom Halls to partake of the bread and wine. A total contradiction in terms. That's another issue that you can discuss with Jehovah's Witnesses if you ever get to talk with them about this subject of the return of our Lord.

Chapter 5

The Nature of Man

This chapter is going to take a look at the subject of the nature of man. When we say "the nature of man," we are talking about the fundamental makeup of man as God designed and made man. Thus, we will be paying particular attention to the use of two Biblical words relating to man: the word "soul" and the word "spirit." We will see how the Bible brings out important information about these two words.

First of all, the Society's definitions of these terms are based upon their analysis of Genesis 1:26 and 2:7. The definition of soul in the Watchtower textbook *Reasoning from the Scriptures*, 1985, p. 375 is as follows:

> In the Bible, "soul" is translated from the Hebrew ne'phesh and the Greek psy•khe'. Bible usage shows the soul to be a person or an animal or the life that a person or an animal enjoys. To many persons, however, "soul" means the immaterial or spirit part of a human being that survives the death of the physical body. Others understand it to be the principle of life. But these latter views are not Bible teachings.

See how emphatic they are against the idea of the soul being an immaterial part of the human that can survive the death of the body. The Watchtower implicitly teaches that the soul is the person!

In harmony with that, they mention Genesis 1:26: "Let us make man in our image, according to our likeness. And let them have in subjection the fish of the sea, and the flying creatures of the heaven...." The Society's definition of being made in God's image and likeness is that it is not a physical resemblance, but it pertains to personality characteristics, moral qualities, attributes, and things like that.

They would illustrate by saying, "Look, the Bible says that God is love, and we have the quality of love; God has infinite intellect, and we have a certain degree of intellect; and so on." "God is a God of justice, and man is capable of exercising justice."

Basically, in that respect, they are pretty much in harmony with the Christian viewpoint. Christian theologians would go along with that. But they go on to teach that, "God is also Spirit, is He not? And, therefore, to be made in the image and likeness of God means that we also have a spiritual element to our nature as well." "We're not just a physical being." In Genesis 2:7, we have a statement about God's procedure in creating man: "Jehovah God proceeded to form man out of the dust of the ground, and to blow into his nostrils the breath of life, and man became a living soul." So, the Society says, "Do you notice how man became a living soul?" "God created this body, and it must have been inanimate for a while; and then Almighty God breathed into it the breath of life, and the result was that man came to life and was animated and could move around, and now he was a living soul." So, their concept of that physical organism, really, is the predominant meaning of the word soul as far as they are concerned.

That brings us to their definition of the word spirit. The Watchtower's conception of the human spirit is that it is just a basic life force; that is to say, rather like electricity. Just as electricity can be put into a machine like a television set, and when the electricity flows through the set, the TV operates, spirit enters the physical organism called man, then we are able to operate too. And this spirit force animates the cells, permeates the cells of the body and makes them function. So, when you die, what happens is that impersonal life force just leaves your body and goes back into the atmosphere.

We want to get into some of the basic Scriptures that talk about these things. I'm going to give you a quotation from *Vine's Expository Dictionary* in which Professor Vine gives his very carefully researched definition of the use of the word soul, especially in the NT Scriptures. He says, "Soul, psuche, has the following definitions and applications:

 1. It refers to the actual life of the body.

That definition would agree with the Society's definition on the basis of Genesis 2:7, that it's the living person, the natural life of the body.

 2. It applies to the immaterial, invisible part of man."

That's very clear, and it's the one the Society would immediately object to.

 3. The word soul is used to denote the seat of personality.

 4. Used to denote the seat of the sentient element in man-that by which he perceives and reflects and feels and desires.

 5. It represents the seat of will and purpose.

 6. It represents the seat of appetite.

The truth of the matter is that the word soul in the Bible has a wide variety of applications. So, it becomes fairly obvious that we would have to determine the particular meaning of the word by looking at its application within its immediate context. The Jehovah's Witnesses have failed to do that. They have come up with one single definition of the word, and apply it to verses that use the word "soul". Translating the Scriptures in that way is dangerous business.

 The word soul does sometimes apply to the human person as a whole. We will commence by looking at some verses that use the word soul to mean the living person. The following verses are all taken from Jehovah's Witness Bible, *The New World Transalation.*

For instance, Genesis 1:20-21, which is applied not to the human realm (perhaps I should not have used the word person) but to the lower life forms. God went on to say, "Let the waters swarm forth with swarms of living souls; and let the flying creatures fly over the earth upon the face of the expanse of the heavens." Verse 21: "God proceeded to create the great sea monsters and every living soul that moves about in the water." The Hebrew word used, is definitely nephesh; and in your Bibles is most likely translated by the word creature, which is a good application in this case because it's definitely talking about the physical object, isn't it? When we're thinking of lower animals and fish of the sea, we're not thinking that the word soul applies to some spiritual element inside them that can survive the death of their physical bodies.

Now, let's look at Exodus 12:16. This was a command given to the people of Israel: "On the first day, there is to take for your holy convention, and on the seventh day a holy convention. No work is to be done on them, only what every soul needs to eat, that alone may be done for you." What does it say in your Bible? Every person? Every man? The word is nephesh in the original Hebrew and can be correctly translated soul. We normally don't think of the soul, that interior element, as eating anything do we? We know that eating is a facility and mechanism of the human physical organism. So, these few verses establish that the word nephesh (soul) is used in the way that the Jehovah's Witness leaders say that it is. But the only thing is that we cannot limit it to that single definition.

It's interesting to examine examples in the Hebrew Scriptures where the word soul is definitely being used with a different connotation. For example, Genesis 35:18. This is talking about the death of Rachel. You might recall from your own Bible studies that Rachel died giving birth to her youngest son Benjamin. So, taking up the account in Genesis 35:18, "Then he [Jacob] pulled away from Bethel; and while there was yet a good stretch of land coming from Ephras, Rachel proceeded to give birth, and it was going hard for her in the delivery. But, so it was, that when it was hard for her in making the delivery, the midwife said to her, 'Do not be afraid, for you will have this son also.' And the result was that as her soul was going out, because she died, she called his name Benoni, but his father called Benjamin."

Did you notice how it said that her soul was going out of her? This was obviously not talking about the physical body itself. It was talking about some other entity that was capable of leaving the body, of going out. And when that soul had left, then the body died. See the point? It is very clear in that passage of Scripture.

Let's look at 2 Kings 4:27, which I think has an interesting usage: "When she came to the man of the true God at the mountain, she at once took hold of him by his feet. At this Gehazi came to push her away, but the man of the true God said, 'Let her alone, for her soul is bitter within her; and Jehovah himself has hidden it from me and has not told me.'" "Her soul was bitter within her." You see, her soul was capable of an emotional response to a situation. Obviously it was not just a bodily response because it said, "her soul within her."

Psalm 107:5 says: "They were hungry and also thirsty; their very soul within them began to faint away." Not just a physical process, but they were depleted to the point that it was affecting their very soul within them.

Jonah 2:7: "When my soul fainted away within me, Jehovah was the one whom I remembered, and then my prayer came into you, into your holy temple." Notice that his soul fainted away within him.

And so, in these verses we see a distinction between the soul and that which is purely the physical organism. The question now is: Could the soul survive the death of the Body? If it is a separate entity, then it should be able not only to leave the body, but it should also be able to survive the death of the body.

For that, we'll use, 1 Kings 17:21-22. This deals with the case when the prophet Elijah was in the home of the widow woman who had a son. While Elijah was staying under her roof and was having the benefit of her hospitality, the boy died. The widow was distraught and wanted Elijah to do something about it. Verses 21-22: "And he proceeded to stretch himself upon the child three times and called to Jehovah, and said, 'Oh Jehovah my God, please cause the soul of this child to come back within him.'" "Finally Jehovah listened to him so that the soul of the child came back in him, and he came to life." This is a very clear and definitive reference to the fact the soul is not only distinct from the human organism, but can literally survive the death of the body and leave the body, and it's capable of coming back into the body once again if God should so wish.

Now, let's come up into the New Testament and take a look at the NT usage of these words. Matthew 10:28 is an interesting example. These are the words of Jesus himself:

> And do not become fearful of those who can kill the
> body but cannot kill the soul. Rather, be in fear of Him
> who can kill both the soul and body in Gehenna.

This is very clear. If the soul were simply the physical organism, then it couldn't be separated from its identity with the body in any way. But according to Jesus, it is possible for men to kill the body and at the same time fail to destroy the soul. However, God can destroy both. He can destroy both soul and body in Gehenna. So, this is a very clear reference showing the distinction in the use of the word soul to refer to some spiritual or interior thing, separate and distinct from the body.

In Acts 2:27, we have another reference. This is the speech of the apostle Peter. Here, he's quoting the words of King David from the Psalms, "Because you will not leave my soul in Hades, and neither will you allow your holy one to see corruption." So there, the writer is speaking of the soul's being in Hades.

How about Acts 20:10? This is the case of the young man named Eutychus sitting in the window in the upper room of the house where Paul was preaching; and Paul was long-winded in preaching. The young man fell asleep and also fell out of the window: "But Paul went downstairs, threw himself upon him and embraced him and said: 'Stop raising a clamor, for his soul is in him.'" In other words, Paul is saying that the soul hasn't left the body, it's OK, he isn't really dead.

I Thessalonians 5:23 will helps us to further define our understanding of the essence and make-up of man. The apostle there is praying for the complete sanctification of Christians. He says that in order for them to be completely sanctified, they need to be sound in soul and body and spirit. And so, the basic makeup of man can be seen to be spirit, which would be at the very heart of our existence; and then the soul; and then the body, the physical organism.

Coming back to the use of the word soul, I want to share with you a little bit more about Vine's definition based upon his analysis of all the Scriptures that use the word. He says,

> Hebrews 4:12 suggests the extreme difficulty in dis-
> tinguishing soul and spirit, because they're so alike in
> their nature and activity.

So, I suggest that we look at Hebrews 4:12 before we carry on with this definition:

> For the word of God is living and active and sharper
> than any two-edged sword, and piercing as far as the divi-
> sion of soul and spirit, of both joints and marrow, and
> able to judge the thoughts and intentions of the heart.

Isn't that an interesting expression? Notice some parallelism there. First of all, the argument of the writer is this: The word of God as a sword is very sharp. So you say, "And how sharp is that?" It is so sharp that it can divide between joints and marrow, and it can even divide between soul and spirit.

So, there is obviously a very close affinity between the soul and spirit, much closer than the affinity between the soul and the body. Therefore, Vine in his definition about that says,

> Generally speaking, the spirit is the higher element; and the soul is the lower element. The spirit may be recognized as the life principle bestowed upon man by God; the soul may be recognized as the resultant life constituted in the individual, the body being the material organism animated by soul and spirit.

It's a little involved but he's really saying that we have one physical element and two spiritual ones. The two spiritual elements are first of all the spirit which is the highest spiritual element, and the soul which is the lowest spiritual element, and then you have the physical body which is the organism that contains both of them. Vine sums it up in this way by saying, "The relationship may be thus summed up: soma (body) and pneuma (spirit) may be separated; but pneuma (spirit) and psyche (soul) can only be distinguished." No separation of spirit and soul, only a distinction in identity between the two, but there is definitely a separation between the spirit and the body at death and the soul and the body at death. So, we should realize from this that the Jehovah's Witness' identity for the word soul is very deficient, and it's far too limited.

I want to look specifically at the meaning and use of the word spirit. For your information, the Hebrew word for spirit is ruach; the Greek term is pneuma. Remembering the Watchtower's definition of the word spirit: it's that which animates the cells of the body, and it's rather like electricity while your body is alive. When your body dies, the spirit removes and goes back into the atmosphere.

On the basis of that, the Jehovah's Witness will take you to Ecclesiastes 3:19-21. (Ecclesiastes is a very popular book with Jehovah's Witnesses.) Let's see what Solomon had to say:

> For the fate of the sons of men and the fate of the beasts is the same. As one dies so dies the other; indeed, they all have the same breath and there is no advantage for man over beast, for all is vanity. All go to the same place. All came from the dust and all return to the dust. Who knows that the spirit of man ascends upward and the spirit of the beast descends downward to the earth?

Some translations use the word breath there instead of spirit. It's the Hebrew word ruach, and it can correctly be translated spirit. However, it can also be translated breath; it's another one of these words that have different applications and meanings.

According to Vine's, you'll see that there are various applications of the Greek word pneuma, which is the equivalent of the Hebrew word ruach. Basically, the thought behind the words is invisibility and force, the ability to do things, to give out power or action.

What are we going to make of this passage the Jehovah's Witnesses use to show that there is not a difference between the spirit of man and the spirit of the beast? They completely fail to understand the book of Ecclesiastes. For some reason it has eluded them as to the very reason why the book of Ecclesiastes was written. The opening statements: "Vanity, vanity, all is vanity..." The word vanity means futility. Everything is worthless; nothing's going anywhere. That's the whole theme of the book of Ecclesiastes; and it was written by Solomon to express what the world of fallen mankind appears to the eyes of the wisest of fallen men.

You see, Solomon was given great wisdom, and he presents the world as he saw it. That's why there are so many references to "I saw," and "behold," and the expression "under the sun" is used many times. He's talking about the condition of fallen mankind in their human natures, leaving God's divine program and God's grace out of the picture. In fact, Solomon in the book of Ecclesiastes doesn't make even the slightest reference to the grace of God or to salvation or to the Messiah or to anything of that nature. He only talks about how things appear to be to mankind, and then every thing is going to end up in judgment.

Look at Ecclesiastes 4:2: "And I congratulated the dead who had already died rather than the living who were still alive." Verse 3: "So better off than both of them is the one who has never existed, who has never seen the evil activity that is done under the sun." Would you talk like that as a Christian? Would you say that expresses your sentiments? Of course not! But it does express the sentiments of fallen mankind who know nothing about the Divine provision of God.

So, we have to understand that this is the viewpoint from which Solomon is writing. In Ecclesiastes 2:1,2: "I said to myself, 'Come now, I will test you with pleasure. So enjoy yourself.' And behold, it too was futility. I said of laughter, 'It is madness,' and of pleasure, 'What does it accomplish?'" Solomon is saying that the situation is so bad that we shouldn't laugh and we shouldn't rejoice, and there shouldn't be any happiness. Verse 11: Thus I considered all my activities which my hands had done and the labor which I had exerted, and behold all was vanity and striving after wind and there was no profit under the sun."

Sadly, we see a very clear picture of how futile and useless human life is when seen from the viewpoint of sinful man who knows nothing about God's grace and salvation and God's divine purpose for the future. The Witnesses have failed to understand that.

Ecclesiastes 3, says, "Who knows about the spirit of man, if it's going up? And the spirit of the animal whether it's going down to the dust of the earth?" Why is it that they don't know? They do not see the activity of the spirit, and so, they can only go by what their eyes see. As Solomon said himself, "I saw..." and "This was the case..." The spirit of man does go somewhere, and it is different from the spirit of the beast, and it does go back to be with its Creator.

With that in mind, let's have a look at some more verses on the spirit. Let's look at Zechariah 12:1: "The burden of the Word of the Lord concerning Israel. Thus declares the Lord who stretches out the heavens, lays the foundation of the earth, and forms the spirit of man within him." "Within" is very emphatic, there, isn't it? The passage identifies where the spirit is. God forms the spirit of man within him.

In Daniel 7:15, Daniel had just received a tremendous vision from the Lord: "As for me, Daniel, my spirit was distressed within on account of it, and the very visions of my head began to frighten me." Notice that it says, "...my spirit was distresses within..." You might be interested to know that the word within that is being used in these passages should literally be translated "inside its sheath." The word in the Hebrew means that the spirit of man exists inside his body like a knife inside its sheath. So, we see a very clear-cut distinction being drawn in these verses by the writers between the spirit of man and his physical structure.

The New Testament teaches further on the spirit and soul of man. Let's take a look at Acts 17:16. This is Paul's speech to the Athenians on Mars' Hill. Before he gets into his great speech, it says, "While Paul was waiting for his fellow Christians in Athens, his spirit within him came to be irritated in beholding that the city was full of idols." His spirit within him got to be irritated because of all the idolatry. The point is that his spirit within him came to be irritated; therefore, the spirit is capable of a response to what is going on outside the person.

Another example is found in 1 Corinthians 2:11: "For who among men knows the things of a man except the spirit of man within him? So too, no one has come to know the things of God except the Spirit of God." Now, the balance is being drawn between two spirits; on the one hand you have the Spirit of God, and on the other hand you have the spirit of man. The question is, "Does the Holy Spirit know the thoughts of God?" Yes He does! And so, in parallel, the one who knows the thoughts of a man is the spirit of man within him.

So, man does have a spirit that is separate and distinct from his body, and that spirit has awareness and knows what's going on. Now, the big question is, "In the NT, do the NT writers reveal that the spirit can survive the death of the body?"

Consider Luke 8, which is an incident that took place during the ministry of Jesus when a little girl died. Jesus went to the house and He brought the little girl back to life. Luke 8:52-55:

> Now they were all weeping and lamenting for her; but He said, 'Stop weeping for she has not died, but is asleep.' And they began laughing at Him, knowing that she had died. He, however, took her by the hand and called, saying, 'Child, arise!' And her spirit returned, and she rose immediately; and He gave orders for something to be given her to eat.

Notice several things about the passage: first of all it says that she was dead. You may ask, "Why, then, did Jesus say that she was asleep?" The reason is that sleep is used as a metaphor for death in the Bible.

The reason sleep is a metaphor for the death of the body is that eventually the body is going to wake up when it is resurrected. Please notice what has to happen in order for the girl to come alive; her spirit had to return. Not some spirit, or for God to send zapping down some more spirit. No, her spirit had to return; it belonged to her; it had her identity.

Another revealing passage is Acts 7:59 where Stephen is being stoned to death. By the way, this passage also says that Stephen fell asleep. Verse 59 says, "And they went on stoning Stephen as he called upon the Lord and said, 'Lord Jesus, receive my spirit!'" Stephen addresses the glorified Lord Jesus in heaven asking Him to do something for him.

He asks Him to receive his spirit into heaven, an impossibility if the spirit is what the Jehovah's Witnesses say it is- just an impersonal life force like electricity that animates the cells of the body.

Lets look at Hebrews 12:22-23:

> But you have come to Mount Zion and to the city of the living God, the heavenly Jerusalem, and to the myriad of angels, to the general assembly and church of the first-born who are enrolled in heaven, and to God, the Judge of all, and to the spirits of righteous men made perfect.

Here, the writer of Hebrews is giving a vision of what it's like in heaven; he's painting a scene, describing the arrangement of heavenly things. Verse 23: "...and to the spirits of righteous men who have been made perfect." We see that collectively, there are, along with the angels and the Lord, the spirits of righteous men made perfect. You see, they've survived the death of the body, and they've gone as Stephen did into the heavenly realm.

The spirit without any doubt survives the death of the body. Does the New Testament show that the soul can do the same thing? We've already had one passage on that, Matthew 10:28:

> Do not become fearful of those who can kill the body but cannot kill the soul; rather, be in fear of Him who can destroy both the body and soul in Gehenna.

It is obvious, according to Jesus, that the soul can remain intact even though the body dies.

By the way, I would like to mention a point. If you show that verse to a Witness, he has a tendency to side-track you by saying, "Hey, look, it says in the end of that verse that God can destroy both soul and body. I thought that the soul was supposed to be immortal; that is, the soul was supposed to go on living; but it says that God can destroy both the soul and body in Gehenna." But you see, what the Witness fails to realize is this: the word destroy in the Greek language of the New Testament does not mean to annihilate or to put totally out of existence; it means to ruin. And so, it's saying that God can take the soul and the body and He's not going to put them out of existence, but He's going to ruin them in Gehenna. However, the soul does survive the death of the body.

We have two final passages: Revelation 6 and Revelation 20. Revelation 6:9-10 reads:

> And when He opened the fifth seal, I saw underneath the altar the souls of those slaughtered because of the Word of God and because of the witness work that they used to have. And they cried with a loud voice to God saying, 'How long, Sovereign Lord, Holy and True, are You refraining from judging and avenging our blood on those that dwell on the earth?'

These people are obviously dead, aren't they? They've been slaughtered; they've been killed as martyrs, and they want to know how long it is going to be until God is going to avenge their blood. But the writer says, "...I saw the souls...of those dead ones, those who had been killed, underneath the altar." Obviously, they had survived the death of the body.

In Revelation 20:4, we have a similar description: "...I saw the souls of those who had been executed with the ax for the witness of Jesus..." He saw the souls once again.

In conclusion, the Society's definition, use and application of the words "soul" and "spirit" in the Holy Scriptures is far too limited. Man truly is an entity that is composed of body, soul, and spirit; and the Bible makes it clear that the spirit and soul can survive the death of the body.

Chapter 6

Death and the Afterlife

The death and afterlife of man ties in very closely with the material that we covered in the previous chap ter. We were taking a look at the Jehovah's Witness definition of man- what we are made of, and who we are. We also considered the Christian definition of man. We decided that we are composed of spirit, soul, and body.

After examining the Jehovah's Witness position concerning the word soul and spirit in the Bible, we were able to see that their application of those words was inadequate. We found that the Witnesses believe that when the physical organism dies, the spirit and soul dies. Nothing survives the death of the body. So that whatever is spiritual, soul or spirit could not apply in any way to any separate or distinct entities within us. Nor would the soul or spirit remain intact and survive the death of our physical organism.

On the other hand, we also found quite a number of Scriptures that clearly teach that the soul and spirit survive the death of the body.

Now we face the question; what happens to a person after death? Let's look at this subject first from the Jehovah's Witnesses' point of view, and then we're going to compare it with the Christian view. We're going to analyze certain important Bible words used in connection with the place that man will go to after death. We're going to look at the Hebrew word Sheol and the Greek word Hades, which are used frequently in the Bible to describe what happens after death.

The Watchtower teaches a very different idea of Sheol. Jehovah's Witnesses base their beliefs on several passages of Scripture. I have selected three of the most prominent passages for your consideration. We're going to look at Ecclesiastes chapter 9. We're going to look at Psalm 146.

And then we will compare these Old Testament passages with what Scripture teaches in the New Testament in John, Chapter 11. We will begin with our consideration of Ecclesiastes, the 9th chapter, verse 5:

> For the living know that they will die, but the dead do not know anything, nor have they any longer a reward for the memory of them is forgotten.

The Witnesses will quote that verse, and verse 10 to reinforce their understanding. Verse 10:

> Whatever your hands find to do, verily, do it with all your might; for there is no activity or planning or wisdom in Sheol where you are going.

Notice please the use of the word Sheol. In the Watchtower Bible that word will appear clearly in verse 10. Some Bibles use the word hell. Some Bibles translate the word grave, which brings us on to a question of the definition of the Hebrew word Sheol.

The Jehovah's Witnesses insist that the word Sheol can only be interpreted in one way when used throughout the Old Testament. If you say to them, what is the interpretation then? They will argue that Sheol is the grave. Sheol is the common grave of mankind, and when you die, the body goes into the grave. It doesn't go down any further than 6 feet, the depth of the grave, and that's the end of you. They say, "Well now, don't these verses back that up?" They're suggesting, for example, in verse 5, "The dead don't know anything," it says, and also again in verse 10, "There's no planning nor wisdom nor activity in Sheol where you're going." The Witnesses say, "There you are, that's a perfect description of the fact that nothing happens after death. Nothing survives, so there's no mental activity, there's nothing going on."

With that in mind, I want to take you back to Ecclesiastes, chapter 9, and point out a few things from that chapter. (we explained the meaning of the book of Ecclesiastes in the chapter, "The Nature of Man.")

I'm going to go back to verse 5, which says that the living know that they will die, and that the dead do not know anything. The verse goes on to say, "nor have they any longer a reward for the memory of them is forgotten." Is that true? Can you make that as a blanket statement concerning all of mankind? You cannot. God has not forgotten them. They're still very much there in the memory of God. They might be forgotten by future generations of mankind, but how about the statement, "neither have they any more reward." Those who were men and women of faith back in the days of King Solomon would be getting their reward of faith would they not. They'll certainly be resurrected along with all other faithful men and women, who share in God's blessings.

Man, however, is limited in what his eyes tell him as well as his understanding. Let's take a look at verse 10 and 11:

> Whatever your hands find to do, thoroughly do with all your might. For there is no activity or planning or wisdom in Sheol where you're going. I saw again under the sun that the race is not to the swift, and the battle is not to the warriors, and neither is bread to the wise, nor wealth to the discerning, nor favor to the men of ability for time and chance overtake them all.

Do you believe that as a Christian? That time and chance overtakes every one of us. Don't you believe that we're in the hands of the Almighty God, and that God maps out our future? But you see from the human viewpoint, from the viewpoint of fallen man, it appears to be a case of time and chance, doesn't it. And that's why gamblers talk about Lady Luck, good fortune and bad fortune. What we need is to gain a proper understanding of Ecclesiastes.

It says in verse six:

> Indeed their love and their hate and their zeal have
> already perished and they will no longer have a share in
> all that's done under the sun.

You cannot say that is a blanket statement of truth about everybody, because there will be some resurrected to share in the blessings that God has for them.

I hope that helps you to get the Book of Ecclesiastes into the correct perspective. You cannot use it my friends to establish a cardinal, fundamental doctrine about what happens to people when they die. We will see the proof of that when we compare it with some important passages in the New Testament.

Now let's consider Psalm 146:3-4:

> Do not trust in princes in mortal man in whom there
> is not salvation. His spirit departs. He returns to the earth
> in that very day his thoughts perish.

Did you catch that point? At the very day of death, at the moment of death, mortal man's thoughts perish. The Jehovah's Witnesses seize on that statement, and they say, "There you are. That shows you that it's all over. There's no more thinking processes for a man who has died. He's gone out of existence." The Witnesses have failed to understand the word "perish" as used in the Bible. Nor do they understand a similar word, the word "destroy", which does not mean to annihilate or to put out of existence. That's not the way the Bible uses that word.

I want to turn you at this point to Vine's Expository Dictionary where we'll consider the word "destroy". Here it tells us that the word destroy is from the same root word as the word "perish". In the Greek, it's "apollumi", and Vine's says this:

> The idea presented by this word is not extinction, but
> ruin; loss, not of being, but of well being.

This is clear from its use, for example, of the spoiling of the wineskins recorded at Luke 5, verse 37. You might remember that Jesus mentioned that as an illustration. He said men do not put new wine into old wineskins, because if you do, the wineskins will perish. This is the same word used in the Greek Scriptures translation of Psalm 146, verse 4. Some Bible translations of the New Testament will say, the wineskins will be destroyed. Now think about it. What really happened to the wineskins? Did they go out of existence? Have the wineskins been annihilated? No. You know what happened. The new wine, which is still fermenting, caused the wineskins to balloon out and finally they rip open at the seams, and they're spoiled for the job for which they were designed. Actually they're still in existence, but they're useless for the purpose for which they were created.

The same thought is contained in Psalm 146, verse 4. When a man dies, if he's an unbeliever, then his thoughts are exposed as ruined, they're of no value, and they accomplish nothing. So that Scripture is not talking about annihilation or going out of existence in any way.

John, chapter 11:11-14 in the New Testament are the words of Jesus himself. This was on the occasion when the friend of the disciples, a man named Lazarus, the brother of Martha and Mary died. Jesus said: 'Our friend Lazarus is fallen asleep, but I go that I may awake him out of sleep.'" The disciples said to Him, "Lord, if he has fallen asleep, he will recover." Now, Jesus had spoken of his death, but they thought that He had spoken of literal sleep. Then Jesus said to them plainly, "Lazarus is dead."

The Witnesses zero in on that passage and on others, which describe death as sleep. They say, "Can't you realize that the physical organism stops functioning? You've gone to sleep, and you don't know anything, you don't feel anything, you don't remember anything, you don't think anything. They totally fail to understand why Jesus and the other Bible writers use the metaphor "sleep". The primary concept behind sleeping is the fact that the one who is asleep is going to wake up eventually. Do you understand the point?

The person who sleeps awakens! So, this is a description of what happens to the physical organism at death. Your body certainly dies, and in effect, goes to sleep. Guess what's going to happen to it. Eventually it's going to wake up again because God's going to call that dead body from its condition of death back into life again.

This Scripture has no reference to what happens to the spirit or soul, you see. Nowhere in Scripture does it talk about the spirit sleeping or the soul sleeping. The references are always to the human body. A good description is found in Daniel 12:2. It says, "Many of those who sleep in the dust of the ground will awake." That's where their bodies have gone. They're sleeping in the dust of the ground, and guess what? They're going to awake in the resurrection. And so none of those passages that the Witnesses use really prove in any definitive sense that there is no spirit and no existence for us after death.

There are, however, verses that speak directly about the death of the believer and the unbeliever in the Old Testament. We'll start at Job 14:13-15. Job is talking about death in this particular passage.

Remember at this time Job was suffering a great deal. He had lost his children and had been inflicted with a severe physical illness. He was feeling much pain and unhappiness, and he appeals to God:

> Oh that thou wouldest hide me in Sheol. [Notice that word again?] ...that thou wouldest set a limit for me and remember me. If a man dies, will he live again? All the days of my struggle I will wait, until my change comes." Thou wilt call, and I will answer Thee; Thou wilt long for the work of Thy hands. (Job 14:13-15)

You see, Job, if we have it correctly, is speaking in terms of death and resurrection. He says, "Hide me in Sheol." Now, that's the word that, more often than not, is translated hell in the KJV, and it is sometimes translated grave. So, we discover in the Old Testament that even righteous men, men such as Job, expected to go to this place called Sheol. (Hell)

Job wasn't the only righteous man that believed in a real afterlife in Sheol. Let's take Genesis 37:5, which is speaking about Jacob, who we recognize to be one of the faithful patriarchs. He was one of the ancestors of the Israelite nation, and a righteous man. Jacob was a man of faith. It says in Genesis 37:35,

> So Jacob tore his clothes, put sackcloth on his loins, and mourned for his son many days, and all his other sons and his daughters arose to comfort him. But he refused to be comforted, and he said, 'Surely I will go down to Sheol [hell] in mourning for my son,' and so his father wept for him.

Now, here's Jacob, a righteous man saying that he's going to go down to Sheol mourning for his son.

That should raise the question: What kind of a place is Sheol if even the righteous persons of the Old Testament go there? Was it just the grave as the Jehovah's Witnesses say, or is there something more to it?

First I want to look at Job 26:5-6. This is talking about death. Job says in verse 5,

> The departed spirits tremble under the waters and their inhabitants. Naked is Sheol before Him, and Abaddon has no covering.

God can see into the depths of Sheol, but how far down is Sheol? It says that it's inhabitants are the departed spirits, and they tremble, and it's under the waters. That doesn't mean in the waters; it means it's below the level of the sea. This is hardly equitable to the six foot down of the common grave. Do you understand what I am saying?

In addition to that is Proverbs 9:17-18. We read:

> Stolen water is sweet; and bread eaten in secret is pleasant. But he does not know that the dead are there, that her guests are in the depths of Sheol.

The Scripture gives the idea that there is something way down there, that it's more than just the common grave of mankind.

Also, consider Deuteronomy 32:22. God is speaking about the nation of Israel and how they brought Him to anger. He puts it this way in verse 22:

> For a fire is kindled in my anger, and burns to the lowest part of Sheol, and consumes the earth with its yield, and sets on fire the foundations of the mountains.

Where are the foundations of the mountains located? Way down in the lower part of the crust of the earth are the foundations of the mountains. And so the context is indicating or conveying the picture of a fiery condition that's existing way down in the lower parts of the earth. It's certainly not the place that one would equate with the common grave of mankind.

Can spirits under any circumstances be raised from that condition? In 1 Samuel 28 we have the case of the witch of Endor. She was the spirit medium that was consulted by King Saul, who wanted to get into contact with a dead person, namely, the prophet of God, Samuel. This woman is raising Samuel as the Scripture says, and Saul speaking to her in verse 14 says, "What is his form?" And she said, "An old man is coming up, and he is wrapped in a robe." "And Saul knew that it was Samuel, and he bowed with his face to the ground and did homage." Note carefully what the spirit of Samuel says to Saul, "Then Samuel said to Saul, 'Why have you disturbed me by bringing me up?'" See that? "...by bringing me up..." out of the place of Sheol is what he is referring to in that passage.

Saul said that he was greatly distressed because the Philistines were waging war against him. He said also, "...God has departed from me and answers me no more." In verse 16, the spirit of Samuel says to him, "Why did you ask me since the Lord has departed from you?" Then Samuel says in verse 18, "Since you did not obey the Lord and execute His fierce wrath upon Amaleck, so the Lord has done this thing to you." "Moreover the Lord will also deliver Israel along with you and your sons into the hands of the Philistines; therefore, tomorrow, you and your sons will be with me."

Indeed, the Lord will give over the army of Israel into the hands of the Philistines. Further on this account we find that Saul and his sons die just as Samuel prophesied. So here, God permitted for His own reasons this situation to take place where the spirit of a dead person could literally be raised from Sheol.

Now, under the heading of Old Testament believers and unbelievers, I'm going to add the account in Luke 16:22. This was obviously a statement made by Jesus in His teaching work. If you look at verse 22, you'll get the whole picture:

> It came about that the poor man was carried away by the angels to Abraham's Bosom, and the rich man also died and was buried, and in Hades he lifted up his eyes...

You might remember the account and say, "Why would you include that passage with those of the Old Testament?" The answer is that although it is in the Gospels, Jesus was speaking at a time when the Old Testament or the Old Covenant was still in force. Everything operated according to God's rules under the Old Covenant, the Mosaic Covenant. That would not change until Jesus died, was risen from the dead, ascended up into heaven, and poured out the Holy Spirit on the day of Pentecost to inaugurate the New Covenant for the Church. Up until then, anyone dying would have to come under the same covenant as the patriarchs and those who died in Old Testament times.

Well, what happened to these men? It says that the rich man went to Hades-notice the use of the word Hades there. "He lifted up his eyes in torment, and he saw Abraham afar off, and Lazarus was with him." So, the two men had gone to the same general locality, and we discover that although they are in the same general area, they are divided by a huge chasm. As we look at it in verse 26, we see that Abraham says that besides all this, there is a great chasm fixed in order that none can pass between the sides.

Amazingly, Jesus is taking the lid off the whole situation with Sheol in the Old Testament. In the Old Testament, all that died went to Sheol. Some, a group of faithful servants of God, their spirits and souls went to a place of comfort. The others on the opposite side of the great chasm went to a place of torment and punishment. Verse 25 of this account brings out the fact that Lazarus was in a place of comfort. Abraham says to the rich man in verse 25:

> Remember how that in you life you received your good things and Lazarus his bad things; and now he is comforted and you are tormented.

We see the real situation after death for those who died in Old Testament times. It is clear that they went to Sheol. Sheol turns out not to be just the grave where the body goes, but it turned out to be an area much further down in the lower regions. Sheol is place with two compartments, as it was, one a place of comfort and one a place of torment.

Now, because we've introduced the word Hades, and we're coming up to the New Testament, I'd like to give you Vine's definition of the word Hades:

> Hades: the region of departed spirits of the lost but including the blessed dead in periods preceding the ascension of Christ. It corresponds to Sheol in the Old Testament.

Please note this: This word Hades never denotes the grave, nor is it the permanent region of the lost. For the appointed time it is for such the intermediate place between decease and the doom of Gehenna.

That's Vine's definition of the word, and certainly its use in the New Testament would bear out what he says.

Now let's consider the death of the unbeliever and the believer in the New Testament. And here, we are going to come across three expressions. We have the word Hades used by Jesus himself in Matthew 11. He's talking to the inhabitants of some of the small villages in the area where He grew up. Their reception of Jesus as a prophet was not a very encouraging reception because they rejected what Jesus had to say. So, on this occasion in Matthew 11:23, we find Jesus making this statement:

> And you, Capernaum, will not be exalted to heaven, will you? You shall descend to Hades; for if the miracles had occurred in Sodom, which occurred in you; it would have remained to this day. Nevertheless, I say to you that it shall be more tolerable for the land of Sodom in the Day of Judgment than for you.

What an incredible thing to say to a village full of people! "Capernaum, you're not going to heaven. You're going to go down to Hades!" The reason why they're going there, according to Christ, is because even the Sodomites would have repented at Christ's miracles, but the people of Capernaum did not. The letter of Jude makes it clear that the inhabitants of Sodom are already undergoing the judicial punishment of eternal fire-isn't that so? So, the future that Jesus is holding out to the inhabitants of this little village of Capernaum isn't a very bright future, but it indicates existence after death and existence under punishment. Now, backing up to verse 21, Jesus includes two other villages:

> Woe to you Chorazin! Woe to you, Bethsaida! For if the miracles had occurred in Tyre and Sidon which occurred in you, they would have repented long ago in sackcloth and ashes. Nevertheless I say to you, it shall be more tolerable for Tyre and Sidon in the Day of Judgment, than for you.

These are very powerful verses indeed. They do not present the concept of just going into eternal non-existence, do they? They don't present the concept of a person dying and just completely going out of existence. That's not what's emerging from these verses.

In addition Romans 2:5 defines God's dealings with the unrepentant,

> But because of your stubbornness and unrepentant heart you are storing up wrath for yourself in the day of wrath and revelation of the righteous judgment of God.

What are these people doing? They're storing up God's Wrath, His anger. How do you store something up? You build it up over a period of time, and it gets bigger and bigger, and more and more. You're storing up a treasure, as it were. So, when the time for the release of God's anger and judgment comes, then you are going to be the recipient of that stored up anger of God.

In verse 9 which shows the results, "There will be tribulation and distress for every soul of man who does evil, of the Jew first, and also of the Greek," How can that be said to be true when you look at the lives of many evil persons? How many die wealthy, at home, and at comfort in their own beds, with nothing on their conscience? Is that true? Of course it is for many evil doers. But Paul says that the unrepentant are building and storing up anger for themselves, and that there's going to be a time when there will be tribulation and distress on their soul. How could such a thing be true if these evil doers are dying in comfort on their own beds, in their own homes, and then going into a condition of nonexistence or annihilation? It doesn't even begin to make sense.

Verse 16 shows that the time of reckoning is the great Day of Judgment: "...on the day when, according to my gospel, God will judge the secrets of men through Christ Jesus." All these verses are clearly indicating what takes place for an unbeliever.

Hebrews 9:27: "And inasmuch as it is appointed for men to die once and after this comes judgment," So, the unbeliever faces judgment when he dies.

Matthew 25:46 emphasizes the destiny of the sheep and the goats at death: "And these will go away into eternal punishment, but the righteous into eternal life." Now, that's a very powerful statement, isn't it? The goats, the unbelievers, the unrepentant go into a condition of eternal punishment; but the righteous, the believers, the repentant go into a condition of eternal life.

The Witnesses found this to be such a difficult passage to deal with that they changed it in their translation. They took the Greek word kolasis; and changed it from "eternal punishment" to "eternal cutting off". This would convey the idea that it was the end of everything for unbelievers forever; there was no experience for them beyond that. However, I'll demonstrate for you shortly that you cannot use the Greek word kolasis that way.

But first we will look at some more verses: Revelation 14:11, which also talks about what happens to the wicked after death. In verses 9-11 we read,

> And another angel, a third one, followed them, saying with a loud voice, 'If anyone worships the beast and his image, and receives a mark on his forehead or upon his hand, he also will drink of the wine of the wrath of God, which is mixed in full strength in the cup of His anger; and he will be tormented with fire and brimstone in the presence of the holy angels and in the presence of the Lamb. And the smoke of their torment goes up forever and ever; and they have no rest day and night, those who worship the beast and his image, and whoever receives the mark of his name.'

That is powerful and frightening language indeed. The Witnesses take that entire passage and they try to treat it as if it were totally symbolic. If you say, "O.K., now of what is it a symbol?" They'll tell you that it is a symbol of annihilation; it's a symbol of going out of existence. My dear friend, that doesn't even begin to make sense, does it?

Look at the words again. It says that they'll be tormented with fire and brimstone, and the smoke of their torment goes up forever and ever; and it says that day and night they have no rest! You can't use an expression like "no rest" to imply a condition of total rest-which is what nonexistence would be. So, this passage is a flat contradiction of the Jehovah's Witness position for people after death; and it is a very powerful testimony for the fact that people do survive the death of the body, and they go into a condition of punishment.

What happens to the believer? The New Testament reveals the believer doesn't have to go down into Sheol like Jacob and Job and Lazarus did. That's not necessary anymore because the Son of Man has opened up the way to heaven. Just a short time after the ascension of Jesus back up into heaven Stephen was giving a great speech to the Jewish leaders. A truthful speech to which they responded by stoning him to death. Take a look at what Stephen said in Acts 7:59:

> And they went on stoning Stephen as he called upon
> the Lord and said, 'Lord Jesus, receive my spirit!'

Stephen knew where his spirit was going to go when his body died. It was going to go to heaven; it was going to be with the Lord Jesus. That's where the spirit of the believer now would go. His body was going to fall asleep, as the next verse says:

> And falling on his knees, he cried out with a loud
> voice, 'Lord, do not hold this sin against them.' And having said this, he fell asleep.

His body died; it fell asleep, and it is now waiting to wake up in the resurrection. His spirit was with the Lord, and his body was asleep.

Okay, let's go to 2 Corinthians 5 where we'll see a little bit more about the death of the believer. Reading from verses 1-9:

> For we know that if the earthly tent which is our house is torn down, we have a building from God, a house not made with hands, eternal in the heavens. For indeed in this house we groan, longing to be clothed with our dwelling from heaven; inasmuch as we, having put it on, shall not be found naked. For indeed while we are in this tent, we groan, being burdened, because we do not want to be unclothed, but to be clothed, in order that what is mortal may be swallowed up by life. Now He who prepared us for this very purpose is God, who gave to us the Spirit as a pledge. Therefore, being always of good courage, and knowing that while we are at home in the body we are absent from the Lord-for we walk by faith, not by sight-we are of good courage, I say, and prefer rather to be absent from the body and to be at home with the Lord.

What's this house that he's talking about in verse 1? It's a metaphor for the body. Yes, the tent and house are metaphors for the body, just as you dwell inside a house. So, Paul is saying that the real me, the inner man, the spirit or the souls dwell inside this tent or this house of my body. In verse 8, "we are of good courage, I say, and prefer rather to be absent from the body and to be at home with the Lord." He's saying that he would rather die so that he could be absent from the body and at home with the Lord. How could he do that if he didn't have a spirit and soul that could survive the death of his body and go to be with Christ? Of course, that's where Paul confidently expected to go.

The same thought is brought out in Phillipians 1. We have Paul the believer speaking about the possibility of dying. He says in verse 21, "For to me, to live is Christ, and to die is gain." Now if Paul is living a life where he can say that for him to live is Christ, that is, his whole life is devoted to Jesus, and he can still say, "even so, for me to die is gain." How could he say that his death would be gain if he, as the Jehovah's Witnesses say, "went into a state of total nothingness and total annihilation."? How could that be gain? He goes on to say that he's undecided about whether he wants to stay with the Christians to help work with them or whether he would rather die and go to be with the Lord. In verses 22-24, we read:

> But if I am to live on in the flesh, this will mean fruitful labor for me; and I do not know which to choose. But I am hard-pressed from both directions, having the desire to depart and be with Christ, for that is very much better; yet to remain on in the flesh is more necessary for your sake. (Phillipians 1:22-24)

The inspired apostle believed that at the moment of his death, he would go to the better condition. He understood at death he would depart and be with Christ. Obviously, Paul knew that there would be some part of him (the spirit or soul) that would survive the death of the body and go to be with Jesus.

In Hebrews 12, we find the writer giving us a vision of the heavenly realm that includes the spirits of the righteous dead. There they are, all up there in heaven with Jesus. In verses 22, 24, we read,

> But you have come to Mount Zion and to the city of the living God, the heavenly Jerusalem, and to myriads of angels, to the general assembly and church of the first born who are enrolled in heaven, and to God, the Judge of all, and to the spirits of righteous men made perfect, and to Jesus, the mediator of a new covenant, and to the sprinkled blood, which speaks better than the blood of Abel.

It is plain to see that the spirits of righteous men are in the presence of Jesus in heaven.

And finally, Revelation 6:9, where again it indicates that the souls of the faithful dead have gone into the heavenly realm. Reading from verse 9:

And when He broke the fifth seal, I saw underneath
the altar the souls of those who had been slain because of
the word of God, and because of the testimony which they
had maintained.

We see here that the soul and spirit of the believer go
to heaven when the physical organism dies.

By the way, direct the Jehovah's Witnesses in their
Bible to Acts 4:21 where the Greek word kolasis is used
again, but this time it doesn't say cutting off. It says punishment.

I want to just say a word about the meaning of the
word torment. The word torment is based on the word
basanismos, and it literally means what it says. It is not a
figurative or imaginative word; it literally means torment.

Chapter 7

The Resurrection

In this particular chapter, I want to invite you to take your Bibles and take an in-depth look at the Jehovah's Witnesses teaching on the subject of the resurrection. This is vital to our knowledge as Christians because it is the resurrection that is one of the key ingredients of the true gospel of salvation and we must be certain that we understand this crucial Biblical doctrine.

I'd like to remind you of a statement made by the apostle Paul as recorded in 1 Cor. the 15th chapter. Reading from verse 1, Paul says,

> Now I make known to you brethren the gospel which I preached to you, and which you also received, in which also you stand, by which also you are saved." And then in verse three he says, "For I delivered to you as of first importance what I also received that Christ died for our sins according to the Scriptures, and that He was buried, and that He was raised on the third day according to the Scriptures. (vv. 1-4)

I think that passage of Scripture makes it abundantly clear that the resurrection of our Lord Jesus and a correct understanding of it is essential to our salvation.

What do the Jehovah's Witnesses actually teach about the resurrection of our Lord? Well basically they say this: "When Jesus died, and he was buried, and his body was placed in the tomb, that body came to its end; and that when Jesus rose from the dead, his body did not rise with him. His body was placed into a condition of nonexistence, if you like. But, certainly, the Jesus that came out of that tomb was not the Jesus who went in, but was a Jesus who existed now in purely spirit form." So, what they're really saying is that Jesus gave up his physical body at death and became purely spirit. Now, I'll think that you'll agree such is a radically different viewpoint than that held by historic Christianity. What we need to do is to compare the two understandings and see which is correct from the Bible's viewpoint.

I don't think that I need to go into extensive detail about the Christian understanding because you're all familiar with that. We believe that Jesus rose physically, bodily, from the dead.

Do Jehovah's Witnesses have any Scriptures upon which they endeavor to base their ideas? The answer is, yes, of course they do. But when we take a look at these Scriptures, I'm sure that we're going to find that there is a misunderstanding on the part of Jehovah's Witnesses as to the meaning of these verses. They have either misunderstood key words, or they have misapplied them, or they have taken the verses out of context.

Let me list the Witnesses' proof texts for you, and then we'll take a look at them. 1 Pet. 3:18, 1 Cor. 15:45, and Heb. 10:10. All these have a bearing on the subject of Christ's resurrection, as we will see.

In addition to these there are a number of other passages we need to mention to you because these support a particular argument that the Watchtower people have used on this subject. The argument goes like this: If you look at the gospel accounts very carefully and the description of what happened after the resurrection of Jesus, you'll see that there were a number of occasions on which Jesus appeared to his own disciples and they didn't recognize him. The Witnesses say, "Now think about that. Look, here were these men and women; these disciples who'd spent more than three years with Jesus. They had followed him; they had sat at his feet to hear his teachings; they had eaten meals with him, etc. And now just a few days after his death and resurrection they no longer recognize him. This must be because Jesus was raised as a spirit, and spirits are invisible, and so, therefore, what Jesus had to do was to materialize different bodies for himself just so His disciples could see him and know that he was there. That would account for the fact that each time he appeared, his own disciples were not able to recognize him. The verses used by Jehovah's Witnesses to support that contention are found at Luke 24:15-16; John 20:14-16; and John 21:4.

Before we take all these passages of Scripture under review, I suggest that we first look at the verses in the Bible which clearly establish the true doctrine of the resurrection of Christ, namely, that he was raised physically from the dead.

We will commence at John 2, reading from verse 18. On this occasion, you might remember, the Jewish people challenged Jesus. If He really was a prophet of God He should be able to give them a spectacular sign. So, they questioned Jesus on those lines. In verse 18 of John 2, we read,

The Jews, therefore, said to Jesus,

> 'What sign do you show us, seeing that you do these things?' Jesus answered and said to them, 'Destroy this temple, and in three days I will raise it up.' The Jews, therefore, said, 'it took 46 years to build this temple, and you will raise it up in three days?' But He was speaking of the temple of His body. When, therefore, He was raised from the dead, His disciples remembered that He had said this, and they believed the Scripture and the word which Jesus had spoken.

That's really very plain and straightforward. The Jews challenged Jesus asking for a sign; and so Jesus said, "Here's a sign for you. Destroy this temple and in three days I will raise it up." Of course the Jews misunderstood what He was getting at. They had imagined that He was talking about that magnificent temple that had been built by Zerubbabel and that had been enlarged by Herod; and, apparently, it had taken 46 years to do. So they said, "Well, it took 46 years to build this temple, and if we break it down, you imagine that you'll raise it up in 3 days?" Jesus, of course, was not talking about that temple at all. What temple was he speaking of? The answer is obvious; He was speaking of the temple of His body; and, of course, it happened that way. He was killed. His temple was broken down.

By the way, it's entirely appropriate that Jesus should refer to his body as a temple because that's a Biblical principle. Whatever God inhabits by Spirit can be considered to be a temple. That's why the Shekinah light shone from between the cherubim over the mercy seat on the Ark of the Covenant inside the original tabernacle. That tabernacle was a temple, a place for God to be. Jesus was obviously referring to His body, when He said, "In three days, I'll raise it up." Now, did it really happen that way? Was Jesus speaking the truth? Of course, the answer is obviously yes!

If we look at the account of the aftermath of the resurrection in Luke 24, we'll see that it's proved beyond doubt. Starting in verse 36, this account deals with an occasion when the disciples were meeting in a room with a closed door, and Jesus appeared in the midst of them. Verse 36:

> While they were telling these things, He himself stood in their midst. They were startled and frightened, and thought they were seeing a spirit. And He said to them, 'Why are you troubled? Why do doubts arise in your heart? See my hands and my feet that it is I myself. Touch me and see, for a spirit does not have flesh and bones as you see that I have.'

That's a truly remarkable account, and it's so definitive that, in itself, it spells the death of this idea of Jehovah's Witnesses that Jesus was not raised bodily or physically from the dead. The whole account is so conclusive. When Jesus appeared in that startling way in the midst of them, it says that they thought that they were beholding a spirit. Well, that's exactly what Jehovah's Witnesses imagine that Jesus was! He was raised as a spirit. And yet Jesus goes to great trouble here in the following verses to point out that He was no such thing. He says to them in verse 39:

> See my hands and my feet. It is I myself. Touch me
> and see, for a spirit does not have flesh and bones as you
> see that I have.

You know, if we take the Jehovah's Witness argument that what Jesus did was to materialize bodies for Himself so that they could see Him, then you must realize that what Jesus would have been doing was carrying out an enormous case of deception. It's easy to see when you think about it, because, He invites His disciples to look at His hands and His feet. Now, why would He want them to look at those particular parts of His anatomy? What's so special about His hands and His feet? The answer is that's where the nail holes were. He was nailed to the cross by His hands and His feet so obviously He was showing them the proof of the crucifixion.

I ask you in all seriousness to put yourselves in the shoes of the disciples. You are meeting in the upper room and all of a sudden, this person appears in the midst of you, and startles you. It's true that your wits would be a little bit befuddled for the moment, but the person who appears starts speaking to you, and says, "Look, it's me. A spirit doesn't have flesh and bones as you see that I have. Take a look at my hands and my feet." And so you do that. You look at the hands carefully, and you look at the feet carefully, and behold, you see the nail holes. Now what's your reaction going to be? Unavoidably you're going to say to yourself, "It's the same Jesus. It's the one whom I saw nailed to the cross. And how do I know it's the same one, that it's the same body literally? Because it has the nail holes in it." You couldn't avoid coming to that conclusion.

Yet, according to Jehovah's Witnesses, it wasn't so at all. Jesus' body was not raised from the dead, and so what he had to do on that occasion was to deliberately manufacture or materialize for Himself a brand new body complete with nail holes in hands and feet. The net result of what Jesus would have done if He had really been raised only as a spirit, was to have completely mislead and confused His disciples because they would be thinking that He got his body back when in reality He didn't. So really, just a little analysis of these verses will show the foolishness of the Jehovah's Witness position on the subject.

OK, let's take another passage, which is very definite on this point. Acts 2. This is the speech of the apostle Peter on the day of Pentecost, and we will take up the account in verse 22 where Peter is making his speech to the people of Israel:

> Men of Israel, listen to these words. Jesus the Nazarene, a man attested to you by God by miracles and wonders and signs which God performed through Him in your midst just as you yourselves know. This man delivered up by the predetermined plan and foreknowledge of God you nailed to a cross by the hands of godless men and put Him to death. And God raised Him up again; putting an end to the agony of death since it was impossible for Him to be held in its power.

Its obvious that Peter is zeroing in on the subject of the resurrection of Jesus Christ. God raised Him up again. We want to know in what condition did God raise Him. In order for Peter to support his thinking, he quotes from King David in the Old Testament. Verse 25:

> For David says of Him [speaking of Jesus], "I was always beholding the Lord in My presence, for He is at my right hand that I may not be shaken; therefore, my heart was glad, and my tongue exalted. Moreover, my flesh also will abide in hope. (Acts 2:25)

Did you notice that prophetic statement by King David, speaking, as it were, the thoughts of Jesus?

Jesus was saying concerning His death, "My flesh also will abide in hope." What hope could there be for the flesh of Jesus if His flesh was not to be raised from the dead? Peter says in verse 27:

"Because thou wilt not abandon my soul to Hades,
nor allow thy Holy One to undergo decay. Thou hast made
known to me the ways of life. Thou wilt make me full of
gladness with Thine presence."

On the basis of that quotation from King David in the
Old Testament, Peter goes on to say this, "Brethren, I may
confidently say to you regarding the patriarch David that
he both died and was buried, and his tomb is with us to this
day." In other words, Peter is saying that David, who uttered these words, died and he was buried...and he's still
buried. He didn't rise from the dead.

Verse 30 goes on to say:

"But because he was a prophet, and knew that God
had sworn to him with an oath to seat one of his descendants upon his throne, he looked ahead and spoke of the
resurrection of the Christ."

You see that? That quotation is very clearly a prophetic
statement concerning the resurrection of Jesus. Now, what
did it say? "My flesh will abide in hope." David looked ahead
and spoke of the resurrection of Christ, that He was not
abandoned to Hades, nor did His flesh suffer decay." This
Jesus God raised up again to which we are all witnesses."
It's perfectly clear. It's definitive. The prophetic Scriptures
foretold that Jesus was to rise bodily, physically from the
dead. And the apostle Peter testifies under the inspiration
of the Holy Spirit that that's exactly what happened.

One further passage of Scripture should be added to
this testimony, and that's taken from the 17th chapter of
the book of Acts, and it's a quotation from the great speech,
which the apostle Paul gave when he visited the city of Athens. The verses, which we have in mind are particularly,
verses 30-32. Paul says,

Therefore, having overlooked the times of ignorance,
God is declaring to man that all everywhere should repent. Because He has fixed a day in which He will judge
the world in righteousness through a man whom He has

appointed, having furnished proof to all men by raising Him from the dead. Now, when they had heard of the resurrection of the dead, some began to sneer, others said, 'We shall hear you again concerning this.'

Obviously then, Paul was talking to the people of Athens about the resurrection of Christ. But notice the way he describes the resurrection in verse 3 and the coming judgment, "God will judge the world in righteousness through a man." Not through a spirit, not through an angel, but through a man. And this is a man whom He has appointed. Furthermore, God has furnished proof to all men by raising Him (that's that man, Jesus) from the dead. Based upon our examination of the foregoing Scriptures we should be able to agree that the physical resurrection of Jesus Christ is well attested to in the Scriptures.

What about these passages that the Witnesses use? Remember them? 1 Pet. 3:18 was the first one. Let's turn our attention to this now and see exactly what the apostle is telling us. Verse 18 reads,

> "For Christ also died for sins once for all, the just for the unjust, in order that He might bring us to God. Having been put to death in the flesh but made alive in the spirit."

Can you see what the Jehovah's Witnesses would argue on the basis of that verse? They'd say, "Well look, it tells you clearly that Jesus was put to death in the flesh, and then He was resurrected in the spirit."

But you know, the question is, is that exactly what that verse is getting at when it says that Jesus was put to death in the flesh but made alive in the spirit? Is that referring to His resurrection? An important part of the problem for Jehovah's Witnesses is this: They don't understand that each human has his own individual spirit, and that spirit survives the death of the body when the body dies. This, of course, applies to Jesus just as much as it does to any other human who has lived on this earth. So, it's not surprising when we look at the account in Luke's gospel, for example, chapter 23:46 which is talking about the moment of Christ's death. It says, "And Jesus, crying out with a loud voice said, 'Father, into Thy hands I commit my spirit.' And having said this, He breathed His last." Notice that statement. Jesus said, "Father, into Thy hands I commit my spirit." The Jehovah's Witnesses' idea is that the spirit that is in humans is merely a kind of basic life force. It's nothing personal; it's something that merely animates the cells of the body. It's rather like electricity flowing into a machine and activating the machine. But that wouldn't make sense for Jesus to say "Father, into Thy hands I commit my spirit" if that's all the spirit in humans really was. Obviously, Jesus recognized that He had something in Him that was special to Him; it was His spirit, and while His body was going to lay dead in the tomb, He was committing that spirit of His into the hands of His Father.

Stephen, by the way, the first Christian to be martyred, did something similar. In Acts 7:59, when they were stoning Stephen to death, the Scripture said, "Stephen prayed, and he said, 'Lord Jesus, receive my spirit.'" And so yes, Jesus had a spirit; Christians have spirits, and those spirits will survive the death of the body. Therefore in 1 Pet. 3:18, this thought of being made alive in the spirit is making a reference to what happened to the spirit of Jesus not what happened to His body.

Furthermore, if we look at verse 19, it will make sense now. It doesn't make much sense to Jehovah's Witnesses, but it says,

> In which also He went and made proclamation to the spirits now in prison who once were disobedient when the patience of God kept waiting in the days of Noah, during which the ark was constructed in which a few, that is eight persons, were brought safely through the water"

When we read the two verses together, looking at the end of verse 18, it says that He was put to death in the flesh, made alive in the spirit, in which He also went and proclaimed to the spirits now in prison. It's referring to His activity during the time in which His body lay dead in the tomb. Jesus in spirit, of course, was active and had some work to do in connection with the spirits in prison. Now, time doesn't permit us to go into a discussion as to which spirits these were and what connection they had with the days of Noah, but it's sufficient to establish the fact that 2nd Peter 3:18 is not specifically referring to the resurrection of Jesus at all.

The Witnesses would say, "Well wait a minute, it does use the expression in verse 18 that Jesus was 'made alive.' Doesn't that expression to be 'made alive' refer to the act of resurrection?" The answer is, yes, sometimes that expression is used to indicate resurrection, but there are times when it doesn't. For example, in Eph. 2 when the apostle was talking about the condition of Christians, before they came into a saving relationship with Jesus Christ, he said that they were dead in their trespasses and sins, and that God had made them alive. In chapter 2:1, we have the statement; "You were dead in your trespasses and sins." And in verse 5, "Even when we were dead in our transgressions, God made us alive together with Christ, by grace you have been saved." It's certainly not a reference to the resurrection, but being brought to life in the eyes of God. So, here we can see clearly that 1 Pet. 3:18 is not a reference specifically to the resurrection of Jesus.

What about the other passages, for example, Heb. 10:10? This has to do with the offering of the body of Christ as a sacrifice. We're all familiar with the references in the Bible to Jesus' being the Lamb of God, which takes away the sins of the world. And, of course, in Hebrews the writer pays a lot of attention to Christ's sacrificial role and the way in which it was prefigured in the Old Testament. In Heb. 10:10 he says,

> By this will [namely, the will of God] we have been sanctified through the offering of the body of Jesus Christ once for all.

In the Watchtower Bible, the NWT, it renders it differently. It says, "We have been sanctified by the offering of the body of Jesus Christ once for all time." The use of the word time there is actually superfluous; it's not in the Greek, and it has been added by the NWT committee for purposes of their own. I guess if you challenged them, they'd probably say for purposes of clarification.

However, reading it correctly, it says, "We are sanctified through the offering of the body of Jesus Christ once for all." All the passage is simply saying is that the body of Jesus just had to be offered once. That's all! One sacrifice was all that was necessary in contrast with the constant repetition of sacrifices under the Jewish law with their priesthood and their animal sacrifices.

The Witnesses try and build a spurious argument on this. They say, "Don't you see that the body of Jesus was offered once for all time? So, therefore, he can't take it back." And on the basis of that kind of reasoning, they do away with the Biblical doctrine of the resurrection. It's all quite clear, though, when we look at the surrounding context of that passage that it's simply saying that Jesus had to offer one sacrifice in contrast with the permanent and repeated sacrifices of Israel.

The other passage I mentioned was in 1 Cor. 15:45. Paul wrote in this verse, "So also it is written, 'The first man, Adam, became a living soul. The last Adam became a life-giving spirit.'" Jesus is more than a body. Jesus is both body and spirit. Jesus' physical body was raised from the grave, and it was raised immortal and incorruptible. But that body also contains a spirit, and it is the spirit inside Jesus that is life giving; not His body. His immortal, incorruptible flesh cannot give life to anything. It is the Spirit, which is life giving (John 6:63).

But that's what is explained to us by the apostle Paul with absolute clarity in Romans 8:9-11 where he says to the Christians:

However, you are not in the flesh but in the spirit if indeed the Spirit of God dwells in you. If anyone does not have the Spirit of Christ, he does not belong to Him; and if Christ is in you, [now, that's obviously not the body of Christ, but the Spirit of Christ] though the body is dead because of sin, yet the spirit is alive because of righteousness.

So, that verse is quite clearly saying that when you become a Christian, and when God comes and dwells in you, He comes to dwell by means of [the] Holy Spirit. And so, even though your body is dead, and it's still dying because of the sin that's in it, even so, your spirit is alive because of Christ. God has declared you righteous in the spirit.

In verse 11, he goes on to say, "If the Spirit of Him who raised Jesus from the dead dwells in you [obviously a reference to the resurrection of Christ; the Holy Spirit, the Spirit of God who raised Jesus from the dead; that Spirit dwells in you the Christian], He who raised Christ Jesus from the dead [in other words, the One who resurrected Jesus Christ] will also give life to your mortal bodies through His Spirit who indwells you." There it is. There's the promise for the Christian.

As a Christian you are now righteous in spirit, if the Spirit of God dwells in you, then that Spirit is going to give life to your mortal body. Now? No, of course not! We've just said, and the facts prove that your body is going to get old and die. It's a reference to your resurrection. When you are resurrected from the dead, you are going to receive a physical resurrection just as Jesus did. And it is at that time that the Holy Spirit, the Spirit of God, the Spirit of Christ gives life to your mortal bodies through the resurrection. So, of course, Jesus is a life-giving Spirit. It's got nothing to do whether He was raised physically with a body or not.

So let's go back and take a careful look at those passages of Scripture where Jesus appeared on several occasions to His disciples after the resurrection, and they did not recognize Him. Luke 24:15-16 was the first account. Two disciples were conversing. Jesus approached them and began traveling with them, but their eyes were prevented from recognizing Him. The Witnesses try and read into that the idea that they couldn't recognize Him because He looked different, because He really didn't have His previous body. He had to materialize some new body for Himself in order to appear to them.

But you see, the Bible is very specific here that their eyes were prevented from recognizing Him. So, obviously, there was some supernatural action by God here. It wasn't that Jesus was looking different; it was just that God was preventing them from recognizing Him. He was holding their eyes, causing some type of preventative measure to take place.

When Jesus had finished preaching His message to these disciples, He entered a house and sat down to eat with them. The Scriptures read in verses 30 and 31,

> It came about that when He had reclined at the table with them, He took the bread and blessed it, and breaking it He began giving it to them, and their eyes were opened, and they recognized Him, and He vanished from their sight.

Again, the Witnesses will say, "You know, it was that familiar gesture of the breaking of the bread that caused them to recognize him." But the Bible is specific again. It says that their eyes were opened. It doesn't say in that verse that due to that familiar gesture, they suddenly caught on to who it was in spite of the fact that He looked different. It says that their eyes, which previously had been prevented from recognizing Him, were now opened to be able to see Him. The Witnesses will also make a big deal of that last statement in verse 31, which says that as soon as they recognized Him He vanished from their sight. They'll say, "Well, there you are, there's the proof that he was a spirit. The moment that they had identified him, he dematerialized, went back to being a spirit again, invisible."

But that is not what the Scripture says. It just says that He vanished from their sight. You see, Jesus could perform miracles. After all, on the first occasion He appeared to His disciples when they were together in that room with the door shut, He appeared in the midst of them. He must have come either through a shut door or through the side of the wall. And that doesn't prove that he was just a spirit. It proves that Jesus has the ability to perform miracles; that's all it proves. After all, if you go back a few years to a period of time during Christ's ministry before He died and before He was resurrected, Jesus did miracles.

Would you believe he walked on the water! Hey, you're not supposed to be able to do that if you have a physical body. Spirits might be able to do it, but physical bodies can't do things like that. Yet, Jesus did it. He walked on the water with His physical body. The fact that He could go through the side of a house or that He could suddenly disappear from them has no bearing at all on whether or not He had a physical body.

The next passage is in John's gospel chapter 20. This is the account of Mary meeting Jesus in the garden. Look at verse 14:

> When she had said this, she turned around and beheld Jesus standing there and did not know that it was Jesus. And Jesus said to her, 'Woman, why are you weeping? Whom are you seeking?' Supposing Him to be the gardener, she said to Him, ...

Obviously, she didn't recognize Him. But if we go back and look at the surrounding context, we see, first of all in verse 1, "...the first day of the week, Mary Magdalene came early to the tomb while it was still dark, and saw the stone already taken away from the tomb." Get the point? It was still dark. So, here she is standing in this garden where the tomb was, in the dark, and she can't see properly. She is not imagining for one second that she is going to bump into Jesus walking around, and so, obviously she didn't recognize Him. But after a short conversation with Jesus, she did.

The account goes on to say in verse 16, "Jesus said to her, 'Mary.' She turned and said to Him, 'Rabboni,' which means teacher." So, when we look at the passage in context, we can see the reason why she couldn't recognize Jesus immediately even though He was the same person and had the same body.

The final account that the Witnesses refer to is in John 21:4. The disciples were getting fed up, and they didn't know what to do. They were discouraged about the future, so they had taken time off to go back to their fishing. In verse 4 while they were in the boat on the Sea of Galilee it says; "but when the day was now breaking, Jesus stood on the beach, yet the disciples did not know that it was Jesus." Point number one, verse 4, "When the day was now breaking..." Notice that it was in the very early dawn hours. It was that time when the light was just breaking; it was turning from night into daytime. Everything at this hour can look indistinct.

On top of that, in verse 8 it tells us how far away from Jesus the disciples were. It says that the other disciples came in the little boat, so they were not far from the land, but about 100 yards away dragging the net full of fish. In actual fact, they were 100 yards off shore. And Jesus appeared on the beach in the very dim light of early dawn, and of course, they didn't recognize Him.

Therefore, rather than proving from these passages that Jesus was a spirit who went around materializing bodies for Himself, they prove, when looked at in their context that conditions were not conducive of clear vision for the disciples. From this we see that the basic fundamental idea that has been presented in these passages of Scripture is clearly: Jesus rose bodily from the dead.

Another point about Christ's resurrection which is extremely important and which the Jehovah's Witnesses entirely overlook is this: that all four gospel accounts record this question of what happened in the tomb. By that I mean that they all record the fact that Jesus when He died, was laid in the tomb, and that when the disciples came sometime afterwards to see the body, the body was no longer there.

All four gospel accounts talk about this, and all four gospel accounts refer to the words of the angels where they say to the disciples, (Mat 28; 6)

"He is not here, for He has risen, just as He said. Come, see the place where He was lying."

The point I'm trying to make is that all four gospel accounts go to considerable length to establish the fact that His body was no longer in the tomb. Think about that. His body was no longer in the tomb is the big deal. The disciples knew only too well that it had been put into the tomb and that a great stone had been rolled over the entrance to the tomb, and so naturally they expected the body to still be there when they went back.

Yet, the angels insisted that the body was no longer there, and the evidence pointed to it. In fact, in Luke's account, the angels even pointed out that no longer is the body there, but the wrapping clothes in which the body was wrapped are still there. You see, this is the whole point; the fact that the body had disappeared was the proof of the resurrection!

If we're going to take the Jehovah's Witness viewpoint, you know what we have to do? We have to say, "Oh well, of course, the body wasn't there because God must have dissolved it into gases, or He must have taken it and miraculously hidden it somewhere." That's total assumption; that's total conjecture. The Bible says nothing about that at all. But the Witnesses have to do that because, otherwise, their whole argument is blown to smithereens. Think about their argument for a minute. This Jesus when He died and His body was laid in the tomb, had finished with His body forever and didn't need it anymore; He was never going to use it again.

He was going to be raised as a spirit. Why couldn't the body have been left in the tomb? You know, after all, Christ was finished with it. So, just let it stay there. It will rot away. It's going to disintegrate like any other body would.

It's no big deal. There's no reason for any angels to come along and remove the body. He was finished with it according to Jehovah's Witnesses. Only the spirit came out according to them.

The whole thing just doesn't make sense if we're going to be honest and we're really going to face up to the true significance of these events. The very fact that every one of the gospel accounts clearly states that the tomb was empty, and that the body had gone, and that Jesus had risen from the dead was proof positive that it was the body that died that also rose again from the dead.

In addition to all the foregoing points, something else should be mentioned. And that is because the Jehovah's Witnesses have totally misinterpreted these Scriptures pertaining to the resurrection of Christ. They've come up with a false doctrine of the resurrection and they have put themselves in a very strange position from a theological and doctrinal point of view. Let me try and illustrate what I mean. You see, if I were in a conversation with an experienced, knowledgeable Jehovah's Witness who knew the teachings of his organization very well, we could have a conversation that would go something like this:

I would say to the Witness, "How was Jesus resurrected?" And the Witness would say, "He was resurrected as a spirit." "Then, what happened to that dead body, that was laid in the tomb?" "Well, God must have either dissolved it into gases, or it was taken by God, and it was hidden away somewhere." Then I would say to him, "Okay now, let me ask you this: Isn't it true of all men that when they die, their body decays and goes back to the dust, and temporarily those men go out of existence. They don't have anything in them that survives the death of their body. There's no preservation of the identity of that individual except, of course, in the memory of God." And the Jehovah's Witness would say, "Well, yes, that's what we believe."

Then I would say, "Well now, does that rule or principle apply to Jesus as well when He died? Did He go out of existence temporarily then? Did He go into a state of nonexistence, because, after all, His body was dead. His body was no good anymore; it didn't function, and there was nothing in Jesus that could go on existing." And the Witness would say, "Yes, that's true." I would have to say, "Then, when Jesus was resurrected, it must not have been His body that was resurrected. As you say it must have been His spirit that was resurrected. Does that mean that God had to recreate Jesus as a spirit? I mean, He'd gone out of existence completely, hadn't He? You're not trying to tell me that the moment His body died, He automatically became an angel again, are you?" And the Witness would have to say, "No" because the Jehovah's Witness leaders don't teach that.

In actual fact, they teach that Jesus Christ was out of existence for three days. He wasn't existing consciously anywhere after His body died. So, the Jehovah's Witness might begin to think now. Yes, he didn't become an angel. The moment he died he went out of existence; therefore, God had to literally recreate him as a spirit. "So, therefore, what was created was brand new, wasn't it? It had never existed before, had it?" And the Witness might say, "Well, you know, it was exactly the same." Yea, but that was not the point. It really was a new creation, wasn't it? The Jesus who had existed no longer existed. So, what God had done was to create a new spirit replacement for Him. That isn't the doctrine of the resurrection.

The idea of the resurrection is not to create something new, but to bring back into existence that which existed before. If perhaps the Jehovah's Witnesses think about it, they'll realize that they really don't believe in the doctrine of the resurrection at all. They have a completely different doctrine. It's a sort of strange, almost mythological doctrine of their own that they've substituted for the true doctrine of the resurrection.

Surely, it's plain to see from the verses that we've considered that what really happened was that when that dead body of Jesus was laid in the tomb; the spirit of Jesus had departed from the body. When the time came for Christ to rise from the dead on the third day, the spirit of Jesus returned to that same dead body and revitalized that same dead body and brought it back to life again, rather in the same way He did when that little girl died.

You might remember that that account is recorded in Luke 8. He brought the spirit of that dead girl back into the body again. I'm going to read this account to you, starting in verse 52. When Jesus had gone into the house, it says that they were all weeping and lamenting for the child. "He said,

> "'Stop weeping, for she has not died, but is asleep.'" And they began laughing at Him, knowing that she had died."

They couldn't understand this expression that Jesus had used when He said that the girl was asleep, because they knew very well that she had died. Verse 54 says,

> Jesus, however, took her by the hand and called saying, 'Child, arise.' And her spirit returned, and she arose immediately, and He gave orders for something to be given to her to eat, and her parents were amazed.

Obviously, this is the same thing that happened to the body of Jesus. His spirit returned, revitalized His body, and that same dead body came to life.

You see, it goes this way: the Witness could now question me as a Christian and say, "Well, if Jesus got his body back, what did he do with that body now that he got it back?" And, of course, my answer as a Christian is that He kept it. The Jehovah's Witness would respond, "Wait a minute. Doesn't the Bible say in Acts 1 that at the end of his ministry and after he'd appeared to the disciples over a period of forty days that he then ascended from the Mount of Olives and left them behind and went back into heaven?"

For example, verse 9 of Acts 1 says:

> After He had said these things, He was lifted up while they were looking on, and a cloud received Him out of their sight. And as they were gazing intently into the sky, behold two men in white clothing stood beside them,

and they also said, 'Men of Galilee, why do you stand looking into the sky. This Jesus who has been taken up from
you to heaven will come in just the same way as you have
watched Him go into heaven.'

The Witnesses will say, "If Jesus had his body back
are you trying to tell us that he took that human body with
him up into heaven?" And the answer is, yes, that's precisely what He did.

If you look at verse 11 very carefully and note the exact words of the angels, they said to the disciples, "This
Jesus [that means the human Jesus, the one with that human body that the disciples were looking at, and could see
going up into the sky] who has been taken up from you will
come in just the same way as you have watched Him go."
The Jesus that went into heaven that took His fleshly, physical body with Him is the Jesus who when He comes again
will come with that same fleshly, physical body.

It is precisely at this point that the minds of Jehovah's
Witnesses begin to boggle. "Oh," they say. "Oh, what nonsense. What are you talking about? What's he going to do
with a human body while he's up in heaven? Human bodies
were created to function on this Earth." It's obviously true
that the human body was designed, along with many other
animal bodies, to function in a planetary environment. I
don't argue with that. There are obviously quite a number
of indications that that is true. But what the Jehovah's Witnesses fail to realize is that the Bible also goes on to show
that the resurrected body of Jesus had been subjected to
four very special changes.

These changes are recorded in 1 Cor. 15:42-43. The
body is raised "imperishable," it is raised "in glory," it is
raised "in power," and it is raised as "a spiritual body."

Now, we had better explain the last one, a "spiritual
body". What's a spiritual body? The Jehovah's Witnesses
are completely confused about that because they think that

a spiritual body is a "spirit body". There's no such thing. A spiritual body is a body, but unlike the natural body. By the way, Adam had a natural body.

Adam's body was a flesh-and-blood body, and functioned according to the flesh-and-blood life cycle. Adam's flesh was corruptible, not immortal. Adam's flesh decayed; and the reason why we know that is that he was given fruit trees in the Garden of Eden so that he could eat food. And what was the purpose of eating food? Was it just a pleasant way of passing the time? Not at all!

The food or fruit was essential to sustaining life in Adam's body. When he ate that fruit, that food went down into his stomach and was attacked by the stomach's digestive juices, which extracted the food materials like vitamins, enzymes, body-building materials, etc., and transferred those food items into the bloodstream. This in turn, fed the muscles and muscle tissues, and the skin, etc., and replaced those cells of Adam's body which would wear out. That's the flesh-and-blood natural body. A spiritual body does not need a blood stream to sustain it. It doesn't need to eat food to keep it in existence because it is sustained by the power of a life-giving spirit within it.

In fact, we've already read the Scripture in Romans 8:11, which said that.

> If now the Spirit of Him who raised Jesus from the dead dwells in you, then He who raised Jesus from the dead will also [now, note this carefully] give life to your mortal bodies by His Spirit which dwells in you.

That's what a spiritual body is. A body no longer sustained by the normal flesh-and-blood method, but it's sustained by the power of an undying spirit within.

Can you see that the body of Jesus, although it's a human body still had essentially undergone four remarkable changes? Remember, that it was raised "imperishable," that it was raised "in glory," it was raised "in power," and it was raised a "spiritual body." Having undergone those four tremendous changes, His body was capable of functioning in an environment that goes way beyond the environment of this planet Earth.

The wonderful thing about this body of Jesus, from the Christian viewpoint, is that the Bible promises that we Christians will eventually receive the same type of body that Jesus has. Remember the passage of Scripture in Philippians 3:20-21, which speaks about the return of our Lord, the calling of the believers to Himself, the raising of the believing dead? It says in verse 20:

> For our citizenship is in heaven from which we also eagerly wait a Savior, the Lord Jesus Christ who will transform the body of our humble state into conformity with the body of His glory by the exertion of the power that He has even to subject all things to Himself.

In conclusion, I would like to suggest in all sincerity that the Jehovah's Witnesses do not know the truth about the Biblical doctrine of the resurrection of Christ. And because the doctrine of the resurrection is a key ingredient in the gospel of salvation, then neither can they know the gospel of salvation. Therefore, neither are they saved.

Chapter 8

Sin & Salvation

The subject we are going to examine now is sin and salvation. When we talk about sin from a Jehovah's Witness point of view as well as a Christian point of view, we have to keep in mind what comes as a result of sin. The end product of sin is death. We're going to take a look at sin and its connection with death from the Jehovah's Witness viewpoint and sin with its connection with death from the Christian viewpoint.

From the Jehovah's Witness point of view, sin is inherited and causes death. The Witnesses use that well-known passage of Scripture in Romans 5, verse 12. We'll be using the New American Standard Bible.

> Therefore just as through one man, sin entered into the world and death through sin, so death spread to all men because all sin.

The Witnesses will say yes, that's true. Our first father, our ancestor Adam, sinned. His wife, Eve, sinned, and together they introduced sin into the world, and it was passed on from generation to generation. So it's true that we all do inherit this sin condition with its resulting curse of death.

However, when the Witnesses use the word "death," they are thinking in terms of physical or organic death. Looking at their recent publication called, *Reasoning from the Scriptures*, on page 98, they give us a definition of death:

> The ceasing of all functions of life after breathing, heartbeat, and brain activity stops, the life force gradually ceases to function in the body cells. Death is the opposite of life.

Dear reader, do you understand how restricted that view of the word death is? Their definition is obviously something to do with this organism of ours. This physical entity with the body cells, the brain activity, the heartbeat is all exclusively referencing to what is happening to our physical organism, or the body. That is the limited viewpoint that the Jehovah Witnesses have of death.

We will consider that a little bit more later on in the chapter. The Witnesses agree that because of sin, man dies a physical death and goes into the grave. Man, because of sin is disqualified from God's favor. Man cannot save himself from death. They also quote Psalm 49, verses 7 and 8. Let us examine that as well. It is a well-know passage of Scripture.

In verse 7 of Psalm 49, it says:

> No man can by any means redeem his brother or give
> to God a ransom for him. So the redemption of his soul is
> costly, and he should cease trying forever.

This is a very powerful Scripture. It reads somewhat similarly in the *New World Translation* - the main idea being we do not have the wherewithal, ability or the intrinsic value in ourselves to offer up a ransom to save either our brothers or ourselves from death. We can't do that. So in this respect, the Witnesses are right about the effect of sin.

They go on to say because we cannot save ourselves, we do need someone to pay a ransom for us. This opens the way to introduce the idea of Jesus and His redemptive work. If you examine 1 Timothy 2:5-6, where it talks about the work of Jesus as a mediator, it says,

> For there is one God and one mediator also between
> God and man - the man Christ Jesus who gave Himself
> as a ransom for all, the testimony borne at the proper
> time.

That's how your Bible will read if you read the King James Version or the New American Standard Bible, or the

NIV. But there is a very important difference if you read the *New World Translation* of that verse. In their bible, it says that this man Jesus gave Himself as a corresponding ransom.

That translation is acceptable. *Vine's Expository Dictionary* says:

> LUTRON, a means of loosing from, occurs frequently in Septuagint, [a translation of the Old Testament from Hebrew into Greek] Where it is always used to signify equivalence."

"Corresponding ransom" is not used in most translations of the Bible, but it's essential for the Jehovah's Witnesses to use it, because their whole concept of Christ's redemptive work is that He gave a ransom price that corresponded to something.

The question is, to what did the ransom price of Christ's life correspond. The answer comes back - it corresponded to the perfect life of Adam. So the value of the life of Jesus, our Redeemer, in the eyes of Jehovah's Witnesses, is the equal - exactly - no more and no less than the life of that perfect man, Adam, created in the Garden of Eden.

The Watchtower publication, *"You Can Live Forever in Happiness on Earth"*, which is one of their publications that they use in their Bible study endeavors. Page 63 provides a picture of a pair of scales with Adam on the one side and Jesus on the other. The scales are perfectly balanced, showing the two men were the perfect equal of one another. That concept is false. That concept is not the biblical idea of the ransom that was provided by Jesus.

The Jehovah's Witnesses believe that the death of Jesus, was the ransom price, the death of Christ - opened the way for salvation for mankind. I want you to notice the way this idea is expressed in the Watchtower magazine. In the August 15, 1987 edition of the Watchtower, inside the front cover is the purpose of the Watchtower, it says this:

> It encourages faith in the now-reigning king, Jesus
> Christ, whose shed blood opens the way for mankind to
> gain eternal life.

Notice anything about that? "The shed blood of Jesus opens the way for mankind to gain eternal life.

Now the word *gain* is a somewhat ambiguous word. How does one gain something? Well, we gain it, perhaps by working for it - to earn it. If we work and earn something, it's to our gain - we've gained it. Or we could gain something by being the recipient of it - somebody gives us something, so we've gained. So, in other words, the indication in the purpose of the Watchtower is not clear. All we know is that mankind somehow can gain eternal life because of what Jesus did. But it turns out when you pursue the Society's publications a little further that you discover that how they gain eternal life if through hard work - through their work.

I have a Photostat copy of the Watchtower, the 15th of August 1972, page 491. Every Jehovah's Witness went to their Kingdom Hall and studied this material together collectively. The heading the study article was "Working Hard for the Reward of Eternal Life." My dear friends, the expression "eternal life" in the Holy Bible is never, never, never connected with the word "reward." Eternal life is not given as a reward. We're going to look at the Scriptures, which tell us quite clearly and unequivocally that eternal life is given as a free gift.

So the truth of the matter is that the Watchtower Society and the Jehovah's Witnesses have somehow developed an unbiblical kind of theology and mental attitude. They have interpreted Scripture to say that their salvation and eternal life really comes from a combination of what Jesus did, plus their hard work in the service of God. That is a works-righteousness philosophy or works-salvation philosophy, and that does not come from God. That comes from man. We need to understand, therefore, there are some real serious inadequacies in the Society's concept of sin and salvation.

Now let us examine the Christian teaching. In Christianity, it is put forward that sin is inherited, as the JW's stated. We agree with that - Romans 5:12 - Christians accept that. But sin is inherited, and please note, it causes death, both spiritual and physical. That's a much wider, much broader concept of the result of sin than the one that's put forward in the Watchtower's definition.

How do we know that there are two aspects to death for humans? There is physical death - that's true - we all know that because we see people die. But how do we know that there is spiritual death as well? And by the way, which aspect of death is the more important, and which aspect of death comes first? Is it the spiritual or the physical?

Let's examine Genesis 2:17, which talks about God's warning to Adam in the beginning about the coming in of the real possibility of death. Here in Genesis, chapter 2, verses 16 and 17, "The Lord God commanded the man saying,

> From every tree of the Garden you may freely eat, but from the Tree of Knowledge of good and evil, you shall not eat [and here comes the punch line that we're looking for] for in the day that you eat from it, you shall surely die.

Please concentrate on that expression - God did not just say to Adam, "if you eat of the tree, you will die." He didn't just say to him, "if you eat of the tree, you will surely die." He said, "in the day that you eat, you will surely die."

And based on the rest of the Bible, it goes on to show that Adam stayed in existence for many, many years. Doesn't it tell us, for example, in Genesis Chapter 5:5? "So all the days that Adam lived were 930 years, and he died." It's obviously talking about the physical death of Adam. That would be the time when Adam's brain stopped functioning and when his heart stopped beating and when his blood stopped circulating in his veins, and his body no longer was alive, and was presumably placed into the ground. Genesis 5:5 is physical death.

But that's not the primary thought of Genesis 2:17, because God says, "in the day that you eat, you will die." Well, did God mean it, or was God telling a lie? How come Adam could continue on for some 900 years after he sinned when God said to him, "in the day that you eat, you will surely die"? The obvious answer is because Adam died spiritually on that very day. He entered into a condition of spiritual death, which we will understand if we think about it - God is removing the lifeline, as it were, and God is having no direct connection with Adam's spirit at all from the time of that sin onwards. He died spiritually.

Now, when children are born as descendants of Adam, they're born in a condition of spiritual death. That's their lot. If you look up Matthew 8, for example, you will see what appears at first sight to be a very enigmatic statement by Jesus. If you really stop to think about it, you will realize that it's a very significant remark. Matthew, chapter 8, verse 21, "another of the disciples said to Him, Lord, permit me first to go and bury my father." Now he was talking about being a follower of Jesus, but first he had something to do. He had to bury his father. That could have meant literally to bury him, or maybe it could have meant to see him out in his old age, the remaining months and years of his life until he dies; and then the man will be released and free from encumbrances to be the follower of Jesus.

But look at the reply in verse 22. Jesus said to him, "Follow me and allow the dead to bury their dead." Do you get the point? How can dead people bury dead people? Those who are physically dead can't bury anybody, not even themselves. So Jesus was here saying that the people around in general were spiritually dead, even though they were walking around and moving and thinking and doing things, they were in a condition of spiritual death. He was saying to the man, "Let them do the job of physically burying your father when he physically dies." That's what that verse of Scripture means.

But it's a great truth to us, because it shows us the double condition that exists for mankind. We are dead spiritually, and that leads ultimately to physical death. That would also explain Ephesians, chapter 2, regarding Paul's letter to the Church at Ephesus. He's talking about the condition that those Ephesian Christians used to be in before they became believers.

You will notice in Verse 1 - he says (past tense) - "you were dead." How? "In your trespasses and sins." Again in verse 5:

> Even when we were dead in our transgressions, God made us alive together with Christ, and by grace you have been saved and raised us up with Him and seated us with Him in the heavenly places in Christ Jesus.

There the concept is, in the state of unbelief; we are dead in the eyes of God - spiritually dead, severed from the life of God. And when we become believers, it is at that time that we are made alive spiritually and we enter into that living relationship with God.

Now, for some reason, the Society's leaders seem to be very blind to this aspect of the results of sin, this condition of spiritual death. They' are also very confused about the reality of sin. They fail to understand the scope of sin. What I mean by scope is the degree of it, the depth of sin, if you like - the comprehensive nature of sin. They fail to understand it. In fact, in their vocabulary, sin is not a word that is used very frequently. It seems to me, if I remember correctly, looking back on my 30 years with the Witnesses, that we used to talk about "missing the mark of perfection" and "falling short of God's perfect requirements". We would use phrases like that, rather than just simply use the word sin.

I think that's because as Witnesses we did not understand truly the force, the meaning, the power, and the impact of the word. So I want to spend a little time reviewing the nature of sin and its effect upon the human race. For that, I would like to examine Romans, chapter 1. This discusses the all-pervading nature of sin.

Romans 1, starting at verse 29. It's talking about the world in general. It says about people that they are being filled with "all unrighteousness, wickedness, greed, evil, envy, murder, strife, deceit, malice." They are "gossips, slanderers, haters of God, insolent, arrogant, boastful, inventors of evil, disobedient to parents, without understanding, untrustworthy, unloving, unmerciful." Wow, what a list. Somewhat comprehensive, don't you think?

And isn't it interesting to see listed there amongst the crimes of mankind are things that you and I might tend to think are not that big a deal listed right along with the serious sins like "murder" in verse 29. It also talks about being gossips and being a little bit deceitful and also being arrogant and boastful and "disobedient to parents?" Don't you see what God is doing there? In bringing together those qualities, those problems, of human nature, He's showing that as far as disqualification is concerned, every one of those things disqualifies us from a relationship with God.

The list disqualifies us from having God's approval and God's favor and having God grant us eternal life. There is no way that anybody is outside that list. Would you agree? Nobody, in all honesty, could look at the list and say, "Well, I'm not mentioned anywhere there." And the whole idea is that God intends, by this list, to put us all in the same boat together and help us to face up to the fact that we all have the same problem.

Verse 32 shows the result of that condition. "Although they know the ordinance of God, those who practice such things are worthy of death." There it is - those who do any of those things are worthy of death. It says they not only do them, but they give approval to those who practice them.

We should begin to realize that sin is a very, very serious problem for the human family. I want to enlarge on this a bit further, because the Bible does. Turn to Romans, chapter 3, and let's take a look at verse 9 onwards. Paul is talking about Christians who come from a Jewish background and Christians who come from a Gentile background, and he says, "Are we any better than they?" He means we Jews

- are we Jews any better than the Gentiles? Not at all. "For we have already charged that both Jews and Gentiles are all under sin, as it is written."

Notice what the apostle does when he says, "as it is written." He makes a series of quotations from the writings of the Old Testament prophets — the prophet Isaiah, and the Psalms and what the writers of the Old Testament said. Look at some of these things. Verse 10 - "it is written there is how many righteous? None righteous-not even one." So in the whole history of mankind, from Adam on down to the present time - of course it's understood that exception here would be Jesus, because He did not inherit Adam's sin. There is none righteous, not even one, amongst mankind who are descendants of Adam. And that's perfectly true. Sin has disqualified the lot of us.

It says, for example, in verse 12, "All have turned aside, and together they have become useless." Now, I ask you, what does the word useless mean? It means you have got no use for it. You have got this object, and you can't do anything with it. It's not good for anything. When I get to this passage, I usually think of an illustration of a young woman executive having a high position in some business or company somewhere. She is also a mother, and here she is getting ready for a tremendously important dinner — a banquet, a business meeting and a dance all rolled into one. So she's gone out and paid $2,000 for a brand new dress. She has just got changed and is all done up like a dog's dinner - that's probably a British expression and you might wonder what that means - but anyway, it means she's all made up and ready to go out.

So here comes one of the children to see the mother, trips over just a couple of feet in front of her and splashes indelible ink down the front of the dress. The mother hasn't got time to do anything else but to take that dress off and throw it in the corner and go and get her second best dress and put that on and make her way off to the banquet.

When she gets back home at the end of the evening and picks this crumpled dress, this $2000 dress off the floor, what does she say? She says, "It's ruined, it's worthless, it's useless. I can't do a thing with it." And that's how it is that we are useless from God's standpoint for the purpose for which He created us. And sin is the quality or condition that has brought that worthlessness and uselessness about.

In the case of the dress, to be objective about it, we would have to say, "hey, you know, look that ink is only staining 7 or 8 square inches of your dress, lady. If you turn the dress around and look at the back of it, it looks okay." Right? But you and I know the woman is not going to wear the dress anymore, don't we? She doesn't care that the back looks all right. If it's spoiled, it's spoiled, and the thing has become useless.

That's very much like the sin that's in us. We are capable of doing some good things. Jesus acknowledged that of His own disciples. He said "if you, although being wicked, know how to give good gifts to your children. Matt 7:11. " You see? So we're capable of doing a limited amount of good, but the presence of the sin within our nature is that which contaminates and disqualifies us totally in the eyes of God. If we go now to verses 19 and 20 of Romans 3, I think we will see the full extent of this:

> We know that whatever the Law says, it speaks to those who are under the Law that every mouth may be closed and all the world may become accountable to God."

So, there it is - the whole world of mankind, descendants of Adam, without exception, are all accountable to God. Paul then remarks about the Law of Moses. He says, "by the works of the Law no flesh will be justified in God's sight for through the Law comes the knowledge of sin." Through the Ten Commandments, we simply learn just how bad our problem is.

I believe that the Jehovah's Witnesses don't fully understand this. If they did fully understand it, they would then realize that if God is going to save us from our sins and declare us righteous and give us eternal life, then He is going to have to do the whole job Himself. We are not in a fit state to do it. Are you with me? You see, the sin contamination is a disqualification. God has to handle this business of salvation for us right from the beginning, right through to the very end. That way He can make sure that the provision of salvation and eternal life will be reliable for us. Man literally cannot save himself.

We have already looked at the first verses in Romans. But let's consider Romans 4, verse 5. It says:

> But to the one who does not work, but believes in Him who justifies the ungodly, his faith is reckoned his righteousness.

Please notice the tremendous emphasis by the writer about the man who does not work, but believes in Him. And thus, he is justified or declared righteous. God is justifying ungodly people. He's taking sinners like you and me who are totally contaminated and totally disqualified and yet still managing to declare us righteous because of what Jesus did on our behalf and because of our belief in the redemptive work of Christ.

And finally, Romans 5:6 from the New American Standard Bible, "For while we were still helpless, at the right time, Christ died for the ungodly." Please notice - there it is again - what kind of persons did Christ die for? The ungodly. An ungodly person is the very opposite of that which is godly. An ungodly person is a person who is steeped in sin and is the very opposite of what God wants him to be. But Christ died for the ungodly "while we were still helpless." Some bibles use the word "weak" there. But the Greek expression literally means to be weak to the point of outright helplessness; that there is nothing that you can do for yourselves. So God is going to have to do the whole deal. And praise God that He's arranged it that way, because if He didn't, we'd remain forever lost.

Let's add to that Ephesians 2 - and remember we looked at the verses that said we used to be dead in our trespasses and sins - but I want you to notice what it says about us in verse 3. Again, talking about our sin condition before we became Christians, "among them [that's all the rest of the unbelievers] we, too, all formerly lived in the lusts of our flesh, indulging the desires of the flesh and of the mind"- and note this - "and were by nature children of wrath, even as the rest." Do you see the point? When God looked at us before we became believers, He saw us as children of His anger - by nature, we were children of God's anger. That's how it is - that's the sin condition in mankind.

So we have to understand the seriousness of it, the all-pervading nature of sin, and the desperate results that it brings. Only when we realize our helplessness and our total disqualification can we then look eagerly to the remedy that God provides for us in the Person and work of Jesus Christ. That brings us down to verses 8 and 9, note the past tense - "for by grace you have been saved through faith, and that, not of yourselves, it is the gift of God." There it is firmly evidenced that salvation comes as a result of the grace of God. Does it say that? Yes, it does.

What is grace? Well, it's a magnificent word, really, and it is very rich in its meaning, but a simple definition would be "undeserved kindness". Unmerited favor might be another way to put it. Unmerited love, unmerited mercy and forgiveness have been bestowed on us completely undeservingly. God has saved us by grace - not because of anything that we did. And we have to understand that He had to do it that way, because if He made salvation dependent upon us, how many people would get saved? Zero. Nobody.

Everybody is contaminated and disqualified by the presence within them of the sin nature. So God had to find a method of saving us that cut the sin condition out of the picture. The emphasis, then, in verse 9 of Ephesians 2, "not as a result of works that no one should boast." Of course, that's the whole idea. What on earth do you imagine that you have to boast of in your salvation? If God did the whole thing and you didn't do any of it because you couldn't because you were contaminated and disqualified, then when God saves you, you will boast in God and not in yourself. If If you don't understand that, guess what you'll do? You will boast in yourself and the part that you played in finally getting saved and obtaining eternal life.

I can assure you that's how it goes, because Jehovah's Witnesses are a classic example of that position. A total misunderstanding and the mindset of arrogance and boastfulness about works that comes along with it. Let me just illustrate: Jehovah's Witnesses issue each year a yearbook. One of the most important features in the yearbook is a chart of Jehovah's Witness activity in all the different countries of the world. This chart of numbers is compiled because every Jehovah's Witness in every Kingdom Hall in every country of the world is required to turn in a report of the work that he does every month. He turns in the number of hours of preaching he does. He turns in a record of the number of pieces of literature he places and the number of return visits he makes to the homes of the people and so on.

That information is collated together at the Kingdom Hall level. Then it is sent on to the branch headquarters of whatever country he is in. The branch headquarters puts all the reports for the country together, and then they send them on to the headquarters in Brooklyn, New York - the world headquarters - and there all the figures are compiled together.

You open up the Yearbook at the chart of activities and there it is - they will tell you the number of hours of preaching they did right down to the very hour - 375, 465, 279 hours it will say, or something like that. This, my friends, is boasting, is it not? Of course it is. And I remember as a Jehovah's Witness when my friends and I got our Yearbook, the first page we turned to was, guess what? The chart of activity — to see how well we had done, to see how hard we had worked, to see how much literature we had placed. And, of course, to see how many new members we'd gained because of all that activity.

So, a failure to understand the problem of sin and its effect of totally disqualifying us from the favor of God is a serious problem. The failure to realize that when God provided salvation from sin and from death, He did the total job himself from beginning to end, and that was the only way to make it reliable. The Watchtower's failure to realize that has led to the philosophy of works and of human boasting. I hope I've made myself clear. The death of Christ paid what price for sin? The full price for sin. The death of Christ didn't just open up the way for something - the death of Christ did it all.

Colossians 2:9-13 is another very important teaching of Scripture.

> For in Him [Jesus] all the fullness of deity dwells in bodily form.

In Jesus, the man, all the fullness of God dwells bodily. Now, as a result of that, verse 10and 11: "And in Him you have been made complete." He is the head of all rule and authority and also in Him "you were circumcised with a circumcision made without hands." That's the declaration of righteousness, my friends. Just as Abraham's circumcision in the flesh was the outward symbol that God had already inwardly declared him to be righteous, so your circumcision is like that - it's a circumcision of righteousness made without hands. It's done by the Holy Spirit, and you are now righteous. It's through Christ. Verse 12, "and you've been buried with Him in baptism in which you were also raised up with Him through faith in the working of God who raised Him from the dead." So you've died with Jesus, and you've been buried with Christ, and you've been raised from the dead with Jesus to a newness of life now." He goes on in verse 13:

> And when you were dead in your transgressions and the uncircumcision of your flesh, He made you alive together with Him, having forgiven us all our transgressions."

Let me try to explain something to you, my friends. If you are a student of the Word of God, you know that a very important thing that God does for you when you become a believer is He declares you righteous, does He not? He "justifies" you, says the Holy Scripture. You have been declared righteous by God because of your faith. But do you realize something? If God could look at your life span from beginning to end — from the moment you were born, became a believer, and finally died physically, if there was but one sin found that he couldn't forgive you for, then He could never step forward and declare you righteous in the first place. There's no way. Because you would have a sin against your name, and one sin disqualifies. James 2:10 NASB

How many sins did Adam have to perform to get himself disqualified? One - that's right; not 1,101, but one. James says in his letter to the Church, that he who breaks one of God's laws breaks them all. So God, then, if He could see one sin in your life that He was not prepared to forgive, He could never step forward and declare you righteous in the first place, because that would be a denial of His own righteous purpose. Do you see the point?

You've been declared righteous for the simple reason given in Colossians 2:13, all your sins have really been forgiven because of the redemptive work of Jesus Christ. NASB

Now, let's go to Hebrews 10:17,18. It says, according to the terms of the Covenant mentioned in the previous verse:

> This is the Covenant I will make with them after those days, says the Lord. I will put my laws in their heart and upon their mind, I will write them. Their sins and their lawless deeds I will remember no more. Now where there is forgiveness of these things, there is no longer any offering for sin.

How many times did Jesus make the offering for sin? Once. And that offering was valuable enough to cover every sin of all believers from the beginning of the world of man-

kind right through to the end of the age. It has all been
covered by the one single and one and only offering for sin
in Jesus Christ.

As a result of that I want you to see some of the most
important words of the New Testament that apply to us as
believers. "Justification". God declaring us righteous; salvation and eternal life are free gifts and cannot be earned.
Is that true? Let's see.

Justification - Romans, Chapter 3, Verse 24 - "For all
have sinned and fall short of the glory of God." So there we
are back again to the fallen condition of mankind, our total
disqualification. We fall short - not good enough. Verse 24,
"being justified as a gift," says my bible, "through God's
grace." That's what it says. So justification then comes to us
entirely as a free gift.

Now, let's examine Romans 5, verses 16 and 17. It says
there, "but the gift" - now please notice that -

> The gift is not like that which came through the one
> who sinned, for on the one hand, the judgment arose from
> one transgression resulting in condemnation, but on the
> other hand, the free gift arose from many transgressions
> resulting in righteousness.

So there it is - that declaration of righteousness, "justification" comes to us as a free gift because of the redemptive work of Christ.

And by the way, while we're on the subject of this passage in Romans 5, do you remember the balancing act that I
told you about? Adam and Jesus balancing each other out?
This passage of Scripture is a total denial of that false Watchtower concept. Look at Verse 15. "The free gift," it says, "is
not like the transgression." You see that? Not like the transgression of Adam, so we want to know what is the difference?

Well, if by the transgression of the one many died much
more did the grace of God and the gift by the grace of the
one man Jesus Christ abound for many. It's obvious that
the grace of God and the grace of Christ are being catego-

rized there as something of infinitely more value than the transgression of Adam. As we look at verse 17 I think we will begin to see the difference.

> If by the transgression of one man, death reigned through that one, much more those who receive the abundance of grace and the gift of righteousness."

There it is again, the declaration of righteousness is a "gift", and the gift of righteousness will reign in life through the one Jesus Christ.

How many sins of Adam did it take to plunge the whole human race into sin and death? How many ? One. One sin brought about a world of sinners. Since then, each sinner who's been born and lived out their life on earth, hasn't just committed one sin. They've committed thousands upon multiplied thousands of sins - every one of them worthy of earning death for that individual. And don't forget, all the unborn offspring in the loins of that individual as well.

And yet, in spite of the multiplied millions upon billions of sins that have come into existence in this world, each one of them worthy of total disqualification, the ransom sacrifice of Jesus, the redemptive work of Christ is capable of atoning for every one of them. Is that clear? So it is not a balance between Adam and Jesus. It is this - Adam is right down here and Jesus is right up there when it comes to the value of their lives.

All right, justification, then, is a free gift. Is salvation a free gift? Well, we've looked at Ephesians chapter 2 - let's remind ourselves of that - verse 8, "for by grace you have been saved through faith and that not of yourselves, it is the gift of God." It is very clear that salvation is gift.

In Acts 15:11 we have the words of the apostle Peter when he was talking to the council that met to discuss whether Gentile believers should be circumcised or not. In verse 11, Peter says, "but we believe that we are saved through the grace of the Lord Jesus in the same way that they are also." How do we get saved? By the grace of God, and the grace of God comes as a gift.

Finally, eternal life is a free gift.

> For the wages of sin is death, but the free gift of God
> is eternal life in Jesus Christ our Lord. (Romans 6:23)

John 4:10-14 will bring out the same thought. We can see that justification, salvation, and eternal life are all presented in the Holy Scripture as a free gift and cannot be earned by any human works.

I hope you can see the difference now between the philosophy of the Witnesses concerning sin and death and salvation and what the Bible really is presenting on the subject.

Although we are saved through the grace of God by faith, that kind of faith that saves us is also the kind of faith that works, and so there is no such thing as a true Christian who truly has faith in the Lord Jesus Christ who doesn't produce good works or Christian works. (James 2:14-26)

Chapter 9

Blood Transfusions

One of the most egregious of the teachings that have been promulgated by the Watchtower Society is that of their prohibition on blood transfusions. The situation for the Witnesses has been very serious over the last 50 years because of that prohibition. Many thousands of Jehovah's Witnesses have died who otherwise need not have died, even though they were perhaps ill or injured, because of this prohibition of transfusion of blood.

The Witnesses haven't always had this particular teaching. In fact, we can trace the history of the Watchtower Society from the 1870s up to the end of the Second World War, 1945, and there was no prohibition on the transfusion of blood. Then in 1946, the Society started publishing articles in the Watchtower and Awake magazines in which they condemned the use of blood for transfusion purposes. They claimed it was a violation of God's law concerning the sanctity of blood.

This has been quite a horrendous thing in the history of the Watchtower Society since that time. We know that the number of untimely deaths that have taken place among the Witnesses runs into the tens of thousands. We don't know the exact figure, because the Society doesn't keep track of the numbers of all their members that die because of refusal to accept blood.

Most people are familiar with newspaper articles that have been published from time to time reporting the untimely death of a Jehovah's Witness because of their refusal to receive blood. This is very well known. The Witnesses themselves are not concerned about the fact that the blood transfusion issue is such a very unpopular one in society in general and thousands of people view them badly because of their belief. They say, "We're only concerned with carrying out the will of God. We're not concerned with pleasing people in general. We have to be obedient regardless of what the public in general thinks about us; and we are basing our prohibition on blood transfusions on what's revealed in the Scriptures."

There are three primary passages of Scripture that the Witnesses use to justify their position. There are actually more than three, but these three primary passages basically cover this point. One of them is recorded in Genesis, Chapter 9. This prohibition was given when Noah and his sons and their wives came out of the Ark after the Flood. It says in chapter 9, verse 1:

> God blessed Noah and his sons and said to them, be fruitful and multiply and fill the earth and the fear of you and the terror of you should be upon every beast of the earth and on every bird of the sky with everything that creeps on the ground and all the fish of the sea into your hand they are given. Every moving thing that is alive should be food for you. I give it all to you, just as I gave the green plant.

God is reminding Noah that up until the time of the Flood, men were vegetarians. They ate the plant of the field. They did not eat flesh. He says in verse 4:

> Only you shall not eat flesh with its life that is its blood. And surely I will require your life blood from every beast I will require it. And from every man's brother I will require the life of man. Whoever sheds man's blood by man, his blood shall be shed.

So here is a definite prohibition on eating the blood of animals and birds that were now made available for man as an important part of their diet. The Society will jump from there to Leviticus 17 where details of the Mosaic Law are being spelled out. That was part of the Law of Moses to the people of Israel. It says in verse 13:

So when any man from the sons of Israel or from the aliens who sojourn with them in hunting catches a beast or a bird which may be eaten, he shall pour out its blood and cover it with earth. For as for the life of flesh, its blood is identified with its life. Therefore I said to the sons of Israel, "You are not to eat the blood of any flesh for the life of all flesh is its blood. Whoever eats it shall be cut off."

Here again is obviously a very strong prohibition against eating the blood of animals, even though it was quite all right to eat the flesh.

Finally they quote also a Scripture passage from the New Testament; Acts, chapter 15, and they include this as part of the prohibition. It starts in Acts: 15:19. By the way, it's James who's speaking here to the Christians:

Therefore it is my judgment that we do not trouble those who are turning to God from amongst the Gentiles, but that we write to them that they abstain from things contaminated by idols and from fornication and from what is strangled and from blood.

The Watchtower claims this passage presents a prohibition on the use of blood for transfusions. As Christians we have to ask ourselves, does the Watchtower Society correctly understand these verses in the Bible? Are they correctly applying these verses when it comes to the use of transfusing blood? Don't forget, all these verses that we've considered so far have to do with the process of eating blood, and that's definitely prohibited. The big question that we have to consider is, does that prohibition apply to the transfusion of blood? Does it fall under the same principle of the law of God. What is the real truth of the situation?

The Society tries to defend its position in an article in their book called, *Reasoning from the Scriptures*, which was published first in 1985. I'm quoting from the 1989 edition.

In the section on blood they ask, "Is a transfusion really the same as eating blood?" That is the salient question that we've been considering so far. Their comment is this.

> In a hospital when a patient cannot eat through his mouth, he is fed intravenously. Now, would a person who never put blood into his mouth but who accepted blood by a transfusion really be obeying the command to keep abstaining from blood? To use a comparison, consider a man who is told by the doctor that he must abstain from alcohol. Would he be obedient if he was not drinking alcohol, but had it put directly into his veins?

At first hearing that, it's a good point. It's pretty persuasive. But it really isn't. To start off when they say, "in a hospital where a patient cannot eat through his mouth, he is fed intravenously." Blood transfussions are not used to feed the patient. Doctors use other types of solutions that have the needed nutrients within them expressly for the purpose of feeding the body.

So, it's not the same thing. Now, would a person who never put blood into his mouth, but who accepted blood by a transfusion really be obeying the command to keep abstaining from blood? Well, yes! The answer is yes, he would. The abstaining, of course, only goes as far as the eating of blood. We have to get it into that context. That is what the Bible is talking about. When Christians have been told to abstain from blood, it's in the context of abstaining from the actual eating of blood.

Witnesses will frequently consider a blood transfusion the same as intravenous feeding which is certainly inaccurate. If a group of persons had come to visit someone in the hospital and passed a room where a doctor and a nurse are seen standing by another patient's bed. They hear the doctor say to the nurse, "this patient is in urgent need of intravenous feeding." The nurse responds, "yes doctor I'll prepare for him to have a blood transfusion right away." The doctor would most likely fire that nurse for incompetence because blood transfusions are not used for intravenous feeding.

Of course the problem of transfusing of blood was unknown in the days of the disciples back in the 1st Century when the New Testament books were being written. There was no such thing as going to a hospital and having a blood transfusion. The whole question of prohibition had to do with the eating of blood. We need to see it that way. It's not right to come along and take a 20th Century situation where a brand new medical practice has come into existence of transfusing blood and insist that in your opinion, the transfusion of blood is the same as the drinking of blood, as they used to do centuries ago. It isn't. It's not the same principle at all.

Where do the Society's leaders get the authority to impose this idea upon their followers? After all, everybody knows that the leaders of the Society are not medical experts. In fact, most of them received a very poor, rudimentary amount of formal education. What this really boils down to is that the Watchtower leaders are basing their ideas upon statements that are made in the Bible, which they misinterpret. What a terrible thing to think that refusing blood transfussions has been imposed upon millions of followers and families of Jehovah's Witnesses. It's too bad that so many people would allow themselves to be fooled into the thinking that it is God's law; that you must not have transfusions of blood.

The main culprit to foist this "no blood" concept on Jehovah's Witnesses was a Watchtower Society official by the name of Clayton J. Woodworth. In 1919 Woodworth was appointed as editor of a magazine called the *Golden Age,* now known as the *Awake* magazine.

The following quotes from various issues of the *Golden Age* will well illustrate this man's strange mindset:

> There is no food that is the right food for the morning meal. At breakfast is no time to break a fast. Keep up the

daily fast until the noon hour...Drink plenty of water two
hours after each meal; drink none just before eating; and
a small quantity if any at meal time. Good buttermilk is
a health drink at meal times and in between. Do not take
a bath until two hours after eating a meal, nor closer
than an hour before eating. Drink a full glass of water
both before and after the bath. (*Golden Age*, Sept. 9, 1925,
pp. 784-785)

The Watchtower Society back in the 1920's and 1930's,
denied the "germ theory of disease" as a dangerous delu-
sion thought up by "demon worshipping" medical doctors.
The Watchtower actually claimed that disease came as a
result of "wrong vibrations" and the Society even had a special machine they marketed to help the Witnesses medi-
cally. It was called, the "Electronic Radio Biola", which apparently could heal sick people by sending through their
bodies special "radio waves" which would correct those
wrong vibrations that caused the sickness!

In the *Golden Age*, April 22, 1925 pp. 453-454 we read,

"Disease is Wrong Vibration. From what has thus far
been said, it will be apparent to all that any disease is
simply an 'out of tune' condition of some part of the organism. In other words the affected part or the body 'vibrates'
higher or lower than normal...I have named this new
discovery...the Electronic Radio Biola, The Biola automatically diagnoses and treats diseases by the use of electronic
vibrations. The diagnosis is 100 percent correct, rendering better service in this respect than the most experienced diagnostician, and without any attending cost."

What was even more appalling about the claims made
by the Watchtower Society (under Woodworth's guidance)
was that the Electronic Radio Biola could receive a piece of
paper with just a dot of ink on it and then the operator of
the machine could answer, "yes" or "no" to all sort of ques-
tions about the patients health.

Woodworth (and the Society) was against the medical practice of tonsillectomy (having your tonsils surgically removed). The following statement appeared in the *Golden Age*, April 7, 1926, p.438:

> "If any overzealous doctor condemns your tonsils go and commit suicide with a case-knife. It's cheaper and less painful."

My dear Christian friends, I ask you, how could any person in their right mind even consider taking medical advice from Woodworth and the people issuing the Golden Age? Don't forget these people are the ones who later on would prohibit blood transfusions!

C. J. Woodworth was also totally against vaccinations as shown by the following quote from the *Golden Age* of Jan. 5, 1929 p. 502.

> "Thinking people would rather have smallpox than vaccination, because the latter sows seeds of syphilis, cancers, eczema, erysipelas, scrofula, consumption, even leprosy and many other loathsome affections. Hence the practice of vaccinations is a crime, an outrage, and a delusion."

It is well known and fully proven fact that the widespread practice of giving vaccinations to children has saved tens of thousands from contracting killer diseases of various kinds.

Finally, the Society changed its mind. The following information is found in the Watchtower Dec. 15, 1952, p.764:

> After consideration of the matter, it does not appear to us to be in violation of the everlasting covenant made with Noah, as set down in Genesis 9:4, nor contrary to God's related commandment at Leviticus 17:10-14. Most certainly it cannot reasonably or Scripturally be argued and proved that by being vaccinated, the inoculated person is either eating or drinking blood and consuming it as food or receiving a blood transfusion. Vaccination does not

bear any relationship to or any likeness to the intermarriage of angelic "sons of God" with the daughters of men, as described in Genesis 6:1-4. Neither can it be put in the same class as described at Leviticus 18:23,24, which forbids the mingling of humans with animals. It has nothing to do with sex relations.

Please note, dear reader, not one word of apology was ever given to those Witnesses who became seriously ill or who even died because they did not receive protective vaccinations when they were young!

And finally we learn about the Watchtower Society's official view of the medical practice of organ transplant from a question and answer section of the *Watchtower*, Nov. 15, 1967, p. 702;

> "Is there any Scriptural objection to donation one's body for use in medical research or to accepting organs for transplant from such a source? W.L., U.S.A.

> ...When there is a diseased or defective organ, the usual way health is restored is by taking in nutrients. The body uses the food eaten to repair or heal the organ, gradually replacing the cells. When men of science conclude that this normal process will no longer work and they suggest removing the organ and replacing it directly with an organ from another human, this is simply a shortcut. Those who submit to such operations are thus living off the flesh of another human. That is cannibalistic. However, in allowing man to eat animal flesh, Jehovah God did not grant permission for humans to try to perpetuate their lives by cannibalistically taking into their bodies human flesh, whether chewed or in the form of whole organs or body parts taken from others."

Now note their reasoning about what happens when a person receives a donated heart or set of kidneys:

> A peculiar factor sometimes noted is a so-called 'personality transplant.' That is, the recipient in some cases

has seemed to adopt certain personality factors of the person from whom the organ came. One young promiscuous woman who received a kidney from her older, conservative, well-behaved sister, at first seemed very upset. Then she began imitating her sister in much of her conduct. Another patient claimed to receive a changed outlook on life after his kidney transplant. Following a transplant, one mild-tempered man became aggressive like the donor. The problem may be largely or wholly mental. But it is of interest, at least, that the Bible links the kidneys closely with human emotions." (*Watchtower*, Sept. 1, 1975, p. 519)

The Society's prohibition on organ transplants of someone else's heart or kidney as an act of cannibalism first appeared in the *Watchtower* magazine Nov. 15, 1967, pp. 702-704. This remained in force for all JW's until the *Watchtower* issue of March 15, 1980, p.31, a period of Thirteen years. During that time thousands of J.W.'s who needed organ transplants died because of this prohibition.

The Witnesses were so brainwashed that they chose to die rather than break "Jehovah's laws." When the Watchtower rule was rescinded no apologies were ever given by the Society for causing the needless deaths of thousands of JW's during the period 1967-1980!

Dear reader, I appeal to your reasonableness and common sense; who in their right mind would put their confidence in a group of religious leaders with such an appalling record? Yet, to this day, millions of JW's are blindly following the Watchtower's view of blood transfusions.

We need to pray that the Lord will have mercy on these lost souls.

Chapter 10

The Cross

The Watchtower Society teaches that Jesus Christ did not die on a cross. They feel that the cross is a pagan symbol and really should have nothing to do with real Christianity. When they look at the history of the different religious empires, they find the Babylonian civilization had a cross in the shape of a "T", and it represented the god, Tammuz. Then later on, the Roman Empire adopted the cross, but again, it was a pagan symbol.

They feel that because Jesus Christ is the holy and righteous Son of God, Jehovah would not permit his righteous and holy son to be executed on a pagan symbol. Thus, associating Him in some way with paganism.

We need to take a look at the evidence, and to really examine how they arrived at those conclusions. Also, if there is anything wrong with their ideas, point out what the problems are.

First of all, they go to the Holy Bible and notice in the original Greek language the word that has been translated "cross" in most Bibles, is the Greek word, Stauros. They find out, etymologically speaking, that the word simply means "torture stake." So on the basis of that word in Scripture they repudiate the cross insisting it wasn't a cross that Jesus died on - it was a simple upright pole, a trunk of a young tree that had been rammed into a hole in the ground. Jesus would have been nailed to this post.

Of course, if that was the method of Christ's death, it would mean that instead of Him dying with his arms stretched sideways and with a nail in each wrist, He would have had His hands crossed together over His head, and the nail would have gone through the crossed wrists. It's interesting to note in connection with this that every time the Society produces an illustration about the death of Jesus

- and by the way, there are dozens of them repeated in Watchtower literature, He always has His wrists crossed above his head. There is one nail or spike driven through them into the post.

Without any variations, the Society will never show Jesus with His wrists crossed over his head and two nails driven through them. The reason for this is, back in biblical times they didn't have the proficient machinery to make nails in the way we have today, so of course, nails or spikes were hammered out on the anvil. They were rough, crude things. The Witnesses reasoned that if you hung Jesus up on the stake with His palms crossed over His head, and tried to drive two nails through the wrists, they would be so big and clumsy, that they would, of course, smash the ligaments of the wrists and break the bones. The weight of Jesus would bring His head and the top part of His body flopping down.

So just from a point of view of logic, consistent with their belief system, they always show the use of one nail. But there is a problem from a Biblical standpoint, isn't there?

Consider the account in the book of John from the Society's *New World Translation*. We are told on the first occasion when Jesus appeared to His disciples in that upper room, Thomas was not with them. When the disciples said to Thomas, "Hey, we've seen the risen Lord," doubting Thomas refused to believe. John 20:25 says this about Thomas:

> Consequently, the other disciples would say to him, "We have seen the Lord," but he said to them, "unless I see in His hands the print of the nails and stick my finger into the print of the nails and stick my hand into His side, I will certainly not believe."

You notice the use of the word nails is in the plural form — not nail singular in the way the Society depicts Jesus just having that one spike or nail through both wrists. Thomas clearly says, "unless I see in His Hands the print of the nails and stick my finger into the print of the nails..." Those are very powerful hints that Jesus, instead of having His hands crossed over his head, must have been holding them out sideways. Each hand, therefore, received its own nail to hold the wrist to the wood.

But, of course, that would mean that there was a cross member to that torture stake. There is plenty of evidence from history and archaeology to support that thought, so the Witnesses are on very shaky ground here. Their method of reasoning these things out is very shallow. They will point you to the Greek word, "Stauros," and say, "Well, look, it means torture stake, it doesn't mean cross." But what they don't realize is that a cross is a form of torture stake even though it has a cross member, it doesn't stop it from being a torture stake. In fact, I say to Jehovah's Witnesses when I have the opportunity, "You let me nail you up to a cross right now, and you will very rapidly discover that the cross that you've been nailed to is, indeed, a torture stake."

They seem to have tunnel vision. They are not able to sort that out. I'm going to quote now from an article in the *New Illustrated Bible Dictionary* by Thomas Nelson which was published in 1995. I want you to have an idea of what their experts say about it. This is quoting from page 315, talking about the shape of the cross.

> In time, the simple pointed stake first used for execution was modified. The four most important of the resulting crosses are:

> 1) The Latin cross, shaped like a lower-case "t." This is the one on which it seems most likely that Jesus died for our sins because of the notice placed over His head - see Matthew 27, verse 37.

> 2) The second type of cross is the St. Anthony's cross, which has the crossbeam up at the top, shaped like a capital "T" [which by the way was the type of cross that the Babylonians had as part of their worship].

3) The third one is called the St. Andrews cross, which is shaped like a capital "X."

4) The fourth example of the cross is the so-called Greek cross, which has the crossbeam in the center, thus making it shaped like a "plus" sign.

All of these crosses were in use down through the centuries, and all of them certainly fulfilled the function of a torture stake. This article in Thomas Nelson's *New Illustrated Bible Dictionary* goes on to give us quite a lot more information about the cross. I would like to quote some of these things. It says, "Crucifixion on a stake or cross was practiced by the Greeks, notably Alexander the Great, who hung 2,000 people on crosses when the city of Tyre was destroyed. During the period between Greek and Roman control of Palestine, the Jewish ruler, Alexander Genais crucified 800 Pharisees who opposed him. But these executions were condemned as detestable and abnormal by decent-minded people of Genais's day, as well as by the later Jewish historian Josephus. So therefore we are told that historical and archaeological evidence shows that crosses were used for the purpose of execution.
Then it goes on to say:

From the early days of the Roman Republic, death on the cross was used for rebellious slaves and bandits, although Roman citizens were rarely subjected to this method of execution.

The practice continued well beyond the New Testament period as one of the supreme punishments for military and political crimes such as desertion, spying, revealing secrets, rebellion, and sedition. Then following the conversion of Emperor Constantine to Christianity, the cross became a sacred symbol to the Christians, and its use by Romans as a means of torture and death was abolished.

Further details are given in Nelson's Dictionary:

> After being fastened to the crossbeam on the ground with ropes or in rare cases, nails through the wrists, the naked victim was then hoisted with a crossbeam against a standing vertical stake. A block or peg was sometimes fastened to the stake as a crude seat, and the seat was then tied or nailed to the stake...

> The recent discovery near Jerusalem of the bones of a crucifixion victim suggests that the knees were bent out side by side parallel to the crossbeam, and the nail was then driven through the sides of the ankles. Death by suffocation or exhaustion normally followed only after a long period of agonizing pain.

Included in this article is an artist's description of a man from that first century execution. It is believed the drawing is a crucifixion based on the remains of a crucified man from the first century, A. D. discovered in a cave in Jerusalem.

The Witnesses are way out of line here, because not only does the Bible contradict them, but also the findings of history and archaeology. It all comes back to this tunnel vision that the Witnesses have, such as ...the word in the Greek in the Bible means torture stake, so therefore, if it means torture stake, it can't mean a cross. This is such foolishness and such shallowness. We need to be more serious students of history and more serious students of the word of God than that.

When we go back to the early writings of Jehovah's Witnesses, we will find that in the early days of the organization, they did believe that Jesus died on the cross. In fact, they believed that all the way through the administration of Charles Russell, which was from the 1870s right through 1916. The second president, Joseph Rutherford, took over the following year in 1917, and they continued to believe and write that Jesus died on the cross.

Another book published by *The Watchtower Bible and Tract Society* is entitled, T*he Harp of God*, and was written by Joseph Rutherford in the year 1921. I'll be quoting from the 1928 edition. On page 140 we read,

> When Jesus died upon the cross of Calvary, He provided the ransom price because His was the death of a perfect human being exactly corresponding with the perfect man, Adam.

This is a very clear statement - "When Jesus died upon the Cross of Calvary..." So what happened within the period 1929 through to about 1935 that Rutherford started forcibly injecting changes into the system of belief of the Jehovah's Witnesses and changing their understanding of quite a few issues.

One of the changes was in 1931 changing their name from the *International Bible Students' Association* to the name, *Jehovah's Witnesses*. In 1935 Rutherford introduced the two-class system into the Watchtower Society by having divided the Witnesses into the 144,000 on the one hand, who apparently were the only ones to go to heaven, and the rest of the Witnesses on the other hand, who were called the other sheep. The other sheep were told their destiny was to live here on earth so they were called the "earthly class."

In amongst all these changes, Rutherford also introduces the change from the Cross to the torture stake. We have a pretty good idea why he did that. What was it that happened in the history of the Society for Rutherford to suddenly make all these quite substantial changes in the teachings of the Jehovah's Witnesses? Christian students of the Holy Bible who study the Jehovah's Witnesses organization, history, teachings and practices, realize that some pretty serious things were going on in that period from 1921 through 1935.

First of all, the Witnesses had experienced some terrible letdowns because of the failure of prophecy. We notice that between the years 1914 and 1925, the Watchtower leaders, Russell and Rutherford, built up the hopes of the Witnesses that Armageddon was just around the corner. Russell picked 1914 to be the end of the Age. Christ would take over rulership of this world and bring the battle of Armageddon and destroy all of the wicked people and organizations, including all the churches and all the false religions. I trust that turned out to be a false prophecy. 1914 saw the beginning of the first World War, but that of course, did not lead into Armageddon.

Rutherford, who took over the organization in 1917, recalculated the date and came to the conclusion that the correct date was 1918. He published that in the Watchtower magazine. Again, the Witnesses were fooled. They got their hopes up, and of course nothing happened except peace which broke out in 1918. The first World War came to an end. Then Rutherford desperately tried to prophesy another date for Armageddon. He chose the year 1925. He wrote a book in 1918 which was later published, called *Millions Now Living Will Never Die*. In this little book Rutherford confidently predicts that the end of the Age, the end of the world, Armageddon, are all going to come in the year 1925.

The Witnesses who had been terribly let down over the failure of 1914 and then again 1918, were now tremendously disappointed by the failure of 1925. Nothing happened. You have to understand the psychology of the Witnesses. This is the main gangplank of their religion. It's their reason for existing, because they are the proclaimers of the great truth that we're living in the last days and that Armageddon is going to come well within our lifetime.

That has always kept the Witnesses buoyed up and excited, looking forward to these dates. But after three prophetic failures, there was a tremendous amount of discontent in the Jehovah's Witnesses organization. This disappointment and the resulting grumbling of the Witnesses was so strong and so widespread that even Rutherford himself was forced to acknowledge it and mention it in one of his books.

However, all these prophetic failures were causing an upheaval in the Watchtower organization and a tremendous amount of discontent. To allay that, Rutherford was desperate to come up with what he called some new light from the Holy Scriptures. This was obviously intended to settle them down and give them something to be interested in and calm their discontent. He needed to establish in their minds that they really were Jehovah's one true religious organization.

It did have that effect. On the basis of the changes that Rutherford made, the Jehovah's Witnesses would now have new doctrines to identify themselves as proof that they really were the one true religion of God. Because they adopted the name, Jehovah's Witnesses, they consider themselves the true religion. The religion that upholds the true name of the true God, and that is Jehovah; would of course be called Jehovah's Witnesses. None of the other religions of the world called themselves by Jehovah's name, so that was a very important point.

Then came the great "truth" that the cross was a pagan symbol and Jesus actually died on an upright beam (like a telephone pole), which was called in Scripture, a "torture stake."

Then Rutherford introduced neutrality - the Witnesses had to be completely neutral in time of war, so they picked that as another sign that they were the true organization of God. Another sign they picked was that they would not celebrate pagan birthdays such as Christmas, Thanksgiving, etc. They would also become the only religion that would go from door to door consistently, taking the Watchtower message to the people - as the Society says, "The Good News of God's Kingdom." That's four signs, and Rutherford was the one who forced the issue of door-to-door preaching, and insisted that all Witnesses be involved.

Then, of course, the final indicator that they were God's one true religion was the prohibition of blood transfusions - the Witnesses could neither donate blood to help the life of another person who was ill nor could they receive blood in the way of a transfusion. They consider these five indicators as proof that they have the truth. This kind of got them over this tremendous disappointment and disillusionment about the leadership of the Society. It enabled them to pick themselves up, as it were, by their bootstraps and carry on.

However, that's not proof of anything, is it? That doesn't deal with the false idea that Rutherford came up with about the torture stake, if it was a torture stake it couldn't be a cross. The other thing they developed over the years was the attitude that I mentioned earlier about the cross being a pagan symbol. Jehovah would not allow His holy and righteous son to be humiliated by being put to death on a pagan symbol. Needless to say, the Jehovah's Witness leaders were completely wrong once again.

Yes, it was Almighty God's intention that His holy and righteous and sinless Son should not only be subject to the most painful death, but it would also be a humiliating death. What more humiliation for the righteous Son of God than to be identified with a pagan symbol in his death? It tells us in Hebrews, chapter 12, verse 2, from the Society's *New World Translation*:

> As we look intently at the chief agent and perfector of our faith, Jesus, for the joy that was set before him, he endured the torture stake, despising shame, and has sat down at right hand of the throne of God.

What does it mean, that Jesus despises shame? It means that He thought nothing of it - that to suffer a shameful death was no big deal for the Lord Jesus Christ. He was perfectly willing to take that into his stride. So yes, he endured a torture stake, despising shame, and was set down at the right hand of the throne of God. The Holy Bible really vindicates the Christian position, even in that particular matter.

Of course it's also true to say that because the holy and righteous and sinless Son of God died on that pagan symbol, His tremendously important death on that symbol transformed it into a symbol of righteousness. That's why Paul said that he gloried in the cross of Christ. Paul didn't talk about Christ's cross or torture stake as being a symbol of shame. No, Paul preached Christ crucified on a cross. We have every reason as Christians to glory in the cross as the Apostle Paul. We further can recognize the truth about this matter about the method by which Christ died, not being sidetracked into foolish speculations from organizations such as Jehovah's Witnesses.

Chapter 11

Holidays

Most people today are aware of the activity of Jehovah's Witnesses because the Witnesses are very zealous in going into their local communities and calling from door to door. The objective is to get people interested in their message and to eventually be able to convince them to become Jehovah's Witnesses.

JWs have some very different ideas about what Christianity is about, and people are curious about that. They wonder why the Witnesses believe as they do. We're going to focus in on a certain type of belief that the Witnesses have, namely that all the public holidays people observe are displeasing to God, and therefore true servants of God would not observe those holidays. I'm speaking about such holidays as Christmas, Easter, birthdays, Valentine's Day, Thanksgiving. All are shunned by the Watchtower Society.

This surprises people, including Christians. They wonder why on earth the Society has taken that stand. I would like to explain to you what happened in the course of the history of the Watchtower organization to cause them to withdraw from the celebration of public holidays. It's important to know this background information historically about the Society because it throws a lot of light onto their organization and the kind of people they are. Please allow me to give you some historical information concerning these views.

First of all, when the Watchtower Society began in an organized way back in the 1870s, under the leadership of a young man by the name of Charles Taze Russell, they did celebrate all of the traditional holidays such as Christmas and birthdays, Easter and Thanksgiving, etc. They participated just like all the other churches do.

Suddenly, in the period 1925 through 1930, all that got changed. What happened in that period was that Russell had died and a man had taken his position by the name of Joseph Rutherford, known amongst the Witnesses as the Judge. He was the leader of the Watchtower organization, and he was the man who decided what teachings would be put into their literature, into their textbooks, and into their *Watchtower* magazine in particular, (the Watchtower magazine is their main teaching instrument.) So they were dependent upon what Judge Rutherford had to say during that 1925-1930 period.

Rutherford claimed that he had special revelations from the throne of Jehovah to tell him that these public holidays, these holy days, as they really are, were pagan. Therefore, genuine Christians should not celebrate them. True Christians should have pure worship, and yet all these pagan holidays were contaminated. So Rutherford commanded the Witnesses during that period that they had to stop observing them.

In fact, it eventually got to the point where the Witnesses were threatened by the leadership that if any of them did celebrate these contaminated holy days, they would be disfellowshipped, excommunicated from the Watchtower organization. So, of course, that put a lot of fear into the average Jehovah's Witness and made sure that he and his family observed the commands of Judge Rutherford, that they should not partake in any of those celebrations. *

The truth of the matter is that the Watchtower Organization was in a bit of a mess and Jehovah's Witnesses were becoming very, very discouraged over the things that had not taken place. Judge Rutherford started to get pretty desperate. He could imagine that the Witnesses would be deserting the Organization in droves, and that the Watchtower Society would lose most of its support. He had to come up with something that would really catch the attention of the average Witness.

By the way, back in those days, they were still called the *International Bible Students*. They didn't take on the

* Footnote: For the reason why Judge Rutherford introduced all these changes in doctrine, see Chapter 10, "The Cross" pages 166-168

name *Jehovah's Witnesses* until 1931. So here are the Bible Students terribly disappointed and Rutherford is desperate to think up something that will get their attention and take away their thoughts about the failure of the prophecies. That's when he claimed that he had this new light of truth from the throne of Jehovah in heaven.

Rutherford claimed to have been directed to understand that all of these well-known holiday celebrations were in essence pagan celebrations. He explained that holidays were full of pagan false teachings, and they were corrupt. Therefore the true servants of God, Jehovah, if they wished to serve God in spirit and truth, would have to cleanse themselves of these pagan holidays. This would be the only way to worship Jehovah in spirit and truth.

The Witnesses stopped completely. They stopped celebrating Christmas, they stopped celebrating Easter, they stopped celebrating personal birthdays, they stopped celebrating Thanksgiving, and so on. All these well-known holidays were now taboo amongst Jehovah's Witnesses. If any Witness family tried to observe those holidays, and if it was discovered that they were secretly doing so, they would be excommunicated from the Watchtower organization.

You see, the whole idea was dreamt up by Rutherford to take the Witnesses' attention away from these three prophetic failures over a short period of time and to get them occupied with something else. The Witnesses believed it. They gave them reason to be very proud of their Organization because they now had pure worship. God had cleansed their religion of all these false celebrations and all these pagan activities; now they were able to worship Jehovah in spirit and truth.

Thus, they developed a tremendous pride. Right to this very day, you will see that the average Witness has intense pride in the fact that they don't celebrate these pagan festivities. They, in fact, boast about themselves on that issue. They say, "The fact that we don't celebrate Christmas and Easter and birthdays and Mother's Day and Thanksgiving is the proof that we are the one true Organization of God.

So that concept bolstered them up from the 1925s on-ward, up through the 1930s, '40s and so on. They can prove they are the people of God because they don't celebrate these pagan festivities that all the churches and church members celebrate.

The real truth about Jehovah's Witnesses is that when they first started in the 1870s and right up to the time of the mid-1920s, they celebrated Christmas, Easter and Thanksgiving. They never had any qualms about it. They enjoyed those celebrations like anybody else- just like all the other churches.

In fact, for the first fifty years of their existence as a religion, they were cheerfully celebrating all the holy days just like all the members of other churches. Then all of a sudden, this crucial period of time, 1925-1930, all these drastic changes were made.

I hope you can see the significance of that. The record of failed prophecy was going so much against them that they had to have something to get their minds and attentions away from negative thoughts. They needed this positive idea that they had now cleaned up their organization spiritually and that Jehovah was very pleased with them. They would now be able to move forward with God's blessing and everything would be fine. That's the real reason for the change.

I really believe that if the Watchtower leadership had not made those false prophecies between the periods 1914-1925, they wouldn't have seen the need to clean up these so-called pagan holidays. They wouldn't have worried about them - which brings us to another point. We need to think about the celebrations themselves. What is it about those celebrations that the Witnesses discovered through their research that would show them in a bad light?

In recent times, the Watchtower Society published a book called "*Reasoning from the Scriptures,*" which was published in 1985. They listed all their reasons for not celebrating holidays. I will give you some samples of what they discovered. For example, they have a quote from McClintock and *Strong's Encyclopedia of Biblical, Theological, and Eccle-*

siastical Literature which says, "the observance of Christmas is not of divine appointment, nor is it of New Testament origin. The day of Christ's birth cannot be ascertained from the New Testament or indeed from any other source."

Then they have a quote from the *Encyclopedia Americana*:

> The reason for establishing December the 25th as Christmas is somewhat obscure, the day was chosen to correspond to pagan festivals that took place around the time of the Winter Solstice. The festival would also celebrate the rebirth of the sun. The Roman Saturnalia, as it was called, a festival dedicated to Saturn, the God of Agriculture, and to the renewal of the power of the sun....Some Christian customs are thought to be rooted in this ancient pagan theology.

The truth of the matter is, of course, as far as those encyclopedia remarks go, they are correct. When we go back to the times of the early church, in the first few centuries we find no record of the Christians celebrating Christmas. It's obviously a celebration that was started in the church by the church leaders at a later time. Research has shed some light on the origin of Christmas.

The Christian religion began to expand throughout the Roman Empire. The pagan Roman religions that were in force at the time were very worried and very jealous of this growing and powerful Christian movement. Because of this they began to enlarge their own celebrations and to make a big fuss about these pagan activities such as Saturnalia, which did take place over a period of time including the 25th of December. They called it In *Sol Victus*, the victory of the sun - s-u-n.

The church leaders did not want the new converts to their Christian religion being snared back into the pagan celebrations of the Roman empire, so they came up with the bright idea, we're going to celebrate the birthday of the son, not s-u-n. And they did. They picked the 25th of December in order to celebrate the birth of Christ and keep the attention and the allegiance of the new converts to Christianity and away from the pagan celebrations.

I suppose there was a certain amount of practical wisdom in there, but it certainly wasn't an idea that God commanded the church to do. We need to recognize that it is a human invention. No doubt, the church leaders had the best of intentions, but what happened was that as more and more people converted over to, so-called Christianity, the more people found pagan reasons for celebrating the birth of Jesus. That's how the introduction of the German Christmas tree came in, Tannenbaum — they just adopted these pagan ideas into the Christian celebration. As far as the giving of presents and gifts, the early Christians didn't give themselves presents and gifts. They also didn't celebrate the birth of Jesus at all. They celebrated His death and resurrection. That was the important thing to them.

There's a certain amount of factual truth behind the Society's attitude towards celebrations such as Christmas. There's a little heading in this book of theirs that says, "gift giving is a part of the celebration, and stories about Santa Claus and Father Christmas, etc., of course, came in later on. The practice of Christmas gift giving is not based on what was done by the Wise Men. They didn't arrive at the time of Jesus' birth anyway. They gave gifts not to one another, but to the child Jesus, in accord with what was customary when visiting notable persons.

It's too bad that the pagans who claimed to have converted over to Christianity brought these ideas in.

The Jehovah's Witnesses go on to talk about Easter. What is the origin of Easter and the customs associated with it? The *Encyclopedia Britannica* comments:

> There is no indication of the observance of the Easter festival in the New Testament or in the writings of the apostolic fathers.

Then the Catholic Encyclopedia tells us, "a great many pagan customs celebrating the return of spring gravitated to Easter. The egg is the emblem of the germinating life of early spring, the rabbit is a pagan symbol and has always been an emblem of fertility." In his book, The Two Babylons, by Alexander Hislopp, we read, "what means the term Easter itself? It is not a Christian name. It bears its pagan origin on its very forehead. Easter is nothing else than Ashtarte, one of the titles of the pagan queen of Heaven."

Furthermore, the Witnesses discovered that there were only two birthday celebrations in the Bible, and they were two pagan leaders — one in the Old Testament was the Pharaoh of Egypt who celebrated his birthday by having his chief baker hanged. And then in the New Testament, we have the case of Herod Antipas, who celebrated his birthday by having the head of John the Baptist cut off. So, of course, the Witnesses seized upon that and said, "Look, these are pagan leaders - Pharaoh of Egypt and Herod Antipas. We need to avoid doing celebrations that are based upon what these people did."

That's true. That's recorded in the Bible. But also recorded in the Bible about Jesus is the celebration of His birth. Now that happened on the day that He was actually born. These celebrations did not come about on some anniversary of Christ's birth, they took place on the actual day of His birth. You might remember from your reading of the Gospel accounts, "the angels of Heaven appeared and rejoiced; and the shepherds of the fields rejoiced at the birth of the Savior from Heaven." But there's no record in Scripture that each anniversary as every year came around that day of Christ's birth was celebrated. That's because it wasn't.

The Christians of the first few centuries concentrated on celebrating the death and resurrection of Jesus; they didn't do it once a year on an anniversary. They did it frequently - as often as once a week. So it's an entirely different setup. The idea of celebrating the birth of Jesus didn't, of course, come in until about the 4th century. The Christian rulers wanted to catch the attention of new converts.

They did not want the new converts slipping back to pagan celebration. So they invented the birthday celebration for the Son of God at that particular time.

I don't know how the reading of this material will affect you. Are you going to feel like you shouldn't celebrate anyway? That could happen. I don't rule it out. When I was a Jehovah's Witness, I didn't celebrate any of these festivities. To be frank with you, from a personal point of view, the only one of the festivities I really missed was Christmas, because of the friendly attitude that was developed among the people for a short time and the parties and the family get-togethers, etc. I kind of missed that when I was a Witness. But you see, if we're Christians, we do have to face up to the fact of what we're going to do about this truth that the celebrations seem to have a pagan origin and they are full of pagan activities and symbols.

Ultimately, Christians should refrain from doing anything that is definitely pagan in origin, even if they do celebrate. For example, if you celebrate Christmas, are you going to give each other gifts? Or are you going to give gifts to Jesus, which is how it should be. Of course it's very difficult with Christian families where there are children and they're expecting to have gifts.

Some Christian families do have a get-together over the Christmas period and they do sing hymns. That's good, because that keeps Jesus in mind. They also have little parties - nothing extravagant - and they do exchange a few gifts. But what they should do, I think, is also to include a gift for Jesus. We should make an offering to Christ of some kind, either by giving it to church or by giving it to a missionary or giving it to a special ministry. That would be good.

I will never forget a few years ago when a huge sign appeared on the billboards at the sides of the freeways in crowded areas and it advised Christians to remember that "Jesus is the Reason for the Season." If you have some type of celebration of Christmas, you should do it with that in mind, that Jesus is the Reason for the Season.

As far as birthdays are concerned, paying special attention to an individual member of the family and giving them gifts and having a party and things like that, of course it's not commanded in the Bible. The Bible is not interested in that type of thing. But if you do it, you should not take the family members and literally put them up on a pedestal. You should show love to them if you want to celebrate the anniversary of their birthday. Little parties are nice also. But don't turn them into pagan celebrations by giving too much attention and too much adulation to the individual whose birthday it is.

This is an accusation that the Society makes about personal birthdays. "You're taking family members and you're putting them up on a pedestal and you're worshipping them, which is an act of false worship." That's a bit nonsensical. We just get together and show love to the family member and have a good time. I don't think the Bible would condemn us for that.

Incidentally, those two pagan leaders and their birthdays recorded in the Bible were not the only birthdays recorded. In the Book of Job, we're clearly advised that Job's family observed birthdays. If you will turn to Job, chapter 1, you will see in verse 4, "Job's sons used to go and hold a feast in the house of each one on his day. And they would send and invite their three sisters to eat and drink with them." So how do we know that the expression "his day" represents birthdays? The answer comes up in Job chapter 3. It says, "afterwards, Job opened his mouth and cursed his day." That's what the original Hebrew says.

Your Bible might read in English, "he cursed the day of his birth." Because that's what it was talking about. But the expression in the Hebrew was "his day." So, therefore, in Job, chapter 1, when it talks about each of the sons of Job celebrating "his day" it was obviously talking about the anniversary of the day of their birth.

Job's sons are not condemned for doing that. The only question that Job raised about that practice is in chapter 1, verse 5: It says, "it came about when the days of feast had completed their cycle that Job would send and consecrate them." That means consecrating the children by rising up early in the morning and offering burnt offerings according to the number of them all. So Job said "perhaps my sons have sinned and cursed God in their hearts. Thus Job did continually."

In other words, Job who was a prophet and priest for his family, offered up these offerings to God. He did not think the celebration of the son's birthdays was terrible in the eyes of God. He was careful however that "perhaps" during the festivities and the rejoicing that went on during the observation of their birthdays, they would do something that was blasphemous or sin against God.

By the way, they would be drinking wine and it's possible they might have become a little loose tongued during those celebrations and could have said some careless and blasphemous things about God. So Job wasn't taking any chances. If the birthday celebrations themselves had been "an anathema" to God, that he didn't want them and He hated those birthday celebrations, Job wouldn't be able to say "perhaps." So the day of celebration was not an act of sinning by Job's sons as far as Job was concerned. It was a question of how they celebrated them and what they did during the celebrations.

But in all these cases, I think Christians have to think seriously about what we are going to do. Obviously if we have birthdays in the family, we should show love to our family member on their special day by having a party for them and perhaps give gifts, but we shouldn't ever elevate them to the point of worshipping them. I think we would all agree with that. In fact, I don't know any Christian families that do elevate their family members to the point of worship. So we really don't have a problem over birthdays. Jehovah's Witnesses reasoning about birthdays is certainly in error. There is no good reasons in Scripture why they shouldn't celebrate them in a small way.

The thing that makes the Witnesses so inconsistent over things like this is the fact that while they will refrain from celebrating the anniversary of the birth of their family members, they will celebrate the anniversaries of weddings. I can remember when I was a Jehovah's Witness. My parents came to their 25th wedding anniversary, (we kids were grown up by then), we worked together and put on a real feast for our parents on this anniversary of their marriage. We called it the Silver Anniversary. We bought them gifts and objects that were silver plated, and made a big fuss over them. We sure put them up on a pedestal that day, even though we were Jehovah's Witnesses.

Now where do the Witnesses get the idea that it was okay to celebrate wedding anniversaries? They claim they get it from the fact that Jesus and his disciples attended a wedding celebration in the village of Cana in Galilee. You remember the famous occasion where Jesus performed a miracle and turned water into wine? The Witnesses will try and use that occasion to support their idea of continuous (year by year) wedding anniversary celebrations.

Jesus and His disciples were not attending a wedding anniversary. They were attending a wedding - the actual time when the wedding took place and the feast that followed the wedding. There's no record at all that Jesus and his disciples went back each year on that day to Cana in order to celebrate the wedding anniversary. So the Witnesses are totally upside down about these things. It seems as if they can't reason clearly on them. They're contradicting themselves in effect if they say it's not okay to celebrate a family birthday anniversary but it is okay to celebrate a wedding anniversary. It is totally self-contradictory and makes nonsense out of the whole thing.

Chapter 12

Neutrality

Most Christians at one time or another have encountered Jehovah's Witnesses at their door. The Witnesses seem to be well prepared and very knowledgeable on many Biblical subjects. Many Christians have also noticed how proud the Witnesses are of the Organization. After all, their leaders have always taught them very definitively that they represent the one and only true religion in the entire world today. They have been taught that Jehovah's Witnesses are the only ones who have the truth of Holy Scripture.

The leaders of the Watchtower Organization claim to be the faithful and discrete slave whom Jesus referred to in Matthew chapter 24:45-47. They claim that the Governing Body of Jehovah's Witnesses, are collectively the "faithful servant" that Jesus spoke of in those passages. Therefore, it is their job to dispense spiritual food to the household of faith.

Thus, the Witnesses automatically learn that the teachings of the Orthodox churches, which are quite different from the Witnesses, are false teachings. In fact, they're taught that the church leaders within Christendom really don't have any insight into Scripture at all. Only the leaders of Jehovah's Witnesses, the group of men, (about 12) known as the Governing Body, can correctly interpret the Bible. (In recent years the Society has dropped the term "Governing Body," but in practice it is still operating.)

One of their teachings that they're very proud about and if I dare say, very stubborn about, is the question of Christian neutrality. They claim, to the very last man to be neutral in the case of conflict between nations. They will not allow themselves to be involved in the armed forces of any country that they're in. At the moment, the Jehovah's Witnesses live in 234 countries around the world.

Consequently, because so many conflicts break out between nations and different groups, Jehovah's Witnesses have to take this stand on the question of neutrality frequently. They tell the political leaders of their country they have no intention of joining any of the armed forces or supporting the activity in any way. This has led, of course, to some very unfortunate consequences.

In the democratic countries, the worst that's happened to the Witnesses when they've taken their stand of neutrality in time of warfare is that they're put in prison for two or three years. But many times in countries run by dictatorships there have been horrible consequences in taking this stand. They have been treated terribly while imprisoned - beaten up and deprived of food. In some cases, they've been assassinated by firing squads. These men were young men of service age and very often many of them were fathers. They had wives and families, and yet they were going to have to go through this because of their stand in connection with neutrality.

Naturally, Christians would raise the question, "What Scriptures do they use to support themselves in that position?" Well, there are a number, and I list the most prominent ones here. We can start with Matthew 26, verse 52. Jesus was being approached by the enemy, the Roman soldiers, and by Judas. Judas was going to betray Him so that the soldiers could take Him into custody. Jesus had His disciples with Him. In chapter 26, verse 52, it says,

> And behold, one of those who were with Jesus reached and drew out his sword and struck the slave of the high priest and cut off his ear.

We note Jesus' response in verse 52:

> Then Jesus said to him, "Put your sword back into its place, for all who take up the sword shall perish by the sword.

The Society uses that passage to support their position. They say, "Hey, Jesus told his own disciples that all who live by the sword shall perish by the sword." He told His disciples at that time (apparently they did have a couple of swords) they couldn't use them in His defense. So the Witnesses interpret that to mean that Christians cannot defend themselves. The Watchtower leaders teach the Witnesses that it's wrong to go into an army if your country is attacked by another country. They are instructed not to go to its defense because Jesus said all that live by the sword shall perish by the sword.

But there's a problem with their interpretation. This specific situation was all part of God's plan for Jesus to be apprehended by the Roman soldiers at that time. He was to be taken into custody and brought before various rulers for trial, which would lead to His ultimate death on the cross. That was God's preordained plan for Jesus, and the time for it to happen had come. Jesus was doing what He had come to do. He was reprimanding His disciples and in effect saying, "Look, I don't want to be defended at this time."

It goes on to say in verse 53 of Matthew 26,

> Or do you think that I cannot appeal to my Father and He will at once put at my disposal more than twelve legions of angels?

Jesus is saying in effect, "I don't need you guys." I can get twelve legions of angels to defend me if that's what I want. But of course the Word of God had to come true, so He says in the very next verse, verse 54, "How then shall the Scriptures be fulfilled that it must happen this way?" Jesus is telling His disciples, don't interfere with the plan of God, because God's plan cannot be thwarted.

He was telling them you are doing the wrong thing by getting out these swords and defending Me.

Similarly, He said to the Apostle Peter earlier in His ministry, which was recorded in Matthew 16:21,

> "And from that time Jesus Christ began to show His disciples that He must go to Jerusalem and suffer many things from the elders and chief priests and scribes, and be killed and raised up on the third day. And Peter took Him aside and began to rebuke Him, saying, God forbid it, Lord. This shall never happen to you." But Jesus turned to Peter and said, "Get behind Me, Satan, you're a stumbling block to Me for you are not setting your mind on God's interests, but upon man's."

Peter, because of his ignorance and misunderstanding of God's plan for Jesus, tried to stop Jesus from speaking that way. Jesus had to rebuke him. And it's a similar situation in the Garden of Gesthamene in Matthew 26. By the way, it was Peter who took his sword out and cut off the man's ear. Again, it was through his ignorance. He didn't realize that this was all part of the absolutely essential plan of God on behalf of man for his salvation - the death and resurrection of Jesus.

So Jesus wasn't telling them here in Matthew 26 to put their swords up because Christians all the way through history would have to observe neutrality. That's not the point of the passage at all.

By the way, you might like to note this; This is the overriding problem for the leaders of Jehovah's Witnesses when it comes to interpreting the Bible. They have this terrible habit of going to Scripture and finding one verse or sometimes two verses together and lifting them right out of their context and giving them their own interpretation. You can't do that and hope to arrive at the truth of Holy Scripture. Do you see the point? Their misinterpretation illustrates that.

Here's another good example they quote in their book *Reasoning from the Scriptures*, which was published by the *Watchtower Bible and Tract Society* in 1985. It has all their fundamental beliefs laid out in a nutshell.

They quote Isaiah 2:2-4:

> It must occur in the final part of the days that the mountain of the House of Jehovah will become firmly established above the top of the mountains and He will certainly render judgment among the nations and set matters straight respecting many peoples, and they will have to beat their swords into plow shares and their spears into pruning shears. Nation will not lift up sword against nation, and neither will they learn war anymore.

Then they say, "individuals out of all nations must personally decide what course they will pursue. Those who have heeded Jehovah's judgment give evidence that He is their God." Well, again, it's a complete misinterpretation because they ignore the surrounding context of those verses. Unfortunately, this is a regular habit of the Society.

If we go to Isaiah chapter 2 at the beginning of the prophecy, we will see it says in verse 1, "The word which Isaiah, the son of Amos, saw concerning Judah and Jerusalem.

That prophecy, as all students of the Bible know, is a prophecy about the millennial rule of Christ. It's when Christ has totally taken over this world's affairs and He's ruling as the Book of Revelation says, with an iron rod. It means that they are going to have to hammer their swords into plowshares. They're going to have to turn their spears into pruning forks, you see? They don't have any choice once the King has taken over. There is automatically going to be a time of peace for all mankind who live during the millennial Kingdom rule. It's got nothing to do with the present time.

The Watchtower has ripped it out of its context and is trying to apply it now. They were applying that passage all the way through the 20th Century, and at the beginning of the 21st Century, they're still using it and applying it.

The third Scripture they use is 2nd Corinthians 10:3-4. The apostle Paul is writing to the Church and he says:

> Though we walk in the flesh, we do not wage warfare according to what we are in the flesh; the weapons of our warfare are not fleshly but powerful by God for overturning strongly entrenched things.

The Society comments on that passage and interprets it as Paul stating that the Apostles and other early Christians never resorted to fleshly weapons such as swords and clubs or carnal weapons to protect the congregation against false teachings. But Paul wasn't discussing warfare between nations. He was not talking about physical conflicts at all. He was talking purely about spiritual conflicts and how he and his fellow disciples constantly had to battle against false teachers that would bring false ideas and try to deceive the people.

Furthermore, if we go back to that Scripture and look at a few more statements, in 2 Corinthians 10:3-4, we'll notice a couple of other things that are very important. In verse 2 of chapter 10:

> I ask that when I'm present I may not be bold with the confidence with which I propose to be courageous against some who regard us as if we walked according to the flesh. For though we walk in the flesh, we do not war according to the flesh, for the weapons of our warfare are not of the flesh but divinely powerful for the destruction of fortresses."

And then he explains what he means, what these fortresses are.

Verse 5, "We are destroying speculations and every lofty thing raised up against the knowledge of God and we are taking every thought captive to the obedience of Christ." Paul is talking about spiritual battle, and their war against the spiritual fortresses that have been built up by false teachers. These ideas have been built up like fortresses in the minds of the people, and Paul is saying, 'Hey, we're going to overthrow those fortresses. For the weapons of our warfare are not of the flesh, but divinely powerful for the destruction of fortresses which are speculations and every lofty thing raised up against the knowledge of God."

So this has nothing to do with warfare between nations. That's not the subject at all. He's talking purely about the spiritual battle that Christians have against false teachings. But we see the Witnesses have falsely used that to try and support their stand of neutrality when nations are fighting each other.

We have to get these Scriptural truths back into their right context and interpret them correctly so that we know what's really going on. We might ask the question, what is the correct Biblical viewpoint about people being in the armed forces of a country? Are they concerned about it? Can a person not become a Christian if he is in the armed forces? If he is in the armed forces already, does he have to resign from his position in the armed services in order to become a Christian? No, that's not what is presented by the Bible.

If we go to Acts, chapter 10, we find the occasion when Peter was especially commissioned by the Lord to go and preach to the family of Cornelius and take the Gospel to them. Now we ask the question, "Who was Cornelius?" The answer is; he was a Roman army officer. He was a Centurion in charge of a hundred troops. He had quite an authoritative position in the Roman army. Peter preached to Cornelius and his family. From verse 44 we read:

> While Peter was still speaking these words, the Holy Spirit fell upon all those who were listening to the message. And all the circumcised believers [that's all the Jewish believers] who had come with Peter were amazed because the gift of the Holy Spirit had been poured out upon the Gentiles, too. For they were hearing them speaking in tongues and exalting God. Then the Apostle Peter said, 'surely no one can refuse the water for those to be baptized who have received the Holy Spirit just as we did, can he?' And he ordered them to be baptized in the name of Jesus Christ.

It was an immediate baptism following conversion and their reception of the Holy Spirit. Obviously, if it was wrong for a Christian to be in the army, Peter would have advised Cornelius that he was going to have to resign and not have anything to do with the armies of Rome. But of course Peter didn't say that, because it wasn't needed.

Interestingly, Jesus commanded Cornelius and all his family and their friends who had been attending and heard the Gospel to get baptized. Well, that's just the opposite of Jehovah's Witnesses today. If they happen to get a Bible study going with an army officer today and they study with him and he wants to become a Witness he will have to be discharged immediately. They will say to him straight out, "Before you can get baptized, sir, you have to resign your position in the army." They wouldn't even think of baptizing him until he had left the armed forces. So you can see that the outlook of Jehovah's Witnesses is very different from that of the early Christians.

Another example would be the case of the Ethiopian jailer. Do you remember when Paul and Silas were beaten and thrown into the stocks in the prison and then the Ethiopian jailer becomes a believer? Let's look at Acts 16, starting in verse 29:

> The jailer called for lights and rushed in and trembling with fear, he fell down before Paul and Silas and after he brought them out, he said, sirs, 'What must I do to be saved?' And they said believe in the Lord Jesus and you shall be saved - you and your household. And they spoke the word of the Lord to him together with all those who were in the house.

Obviously they told this jailer the Gospel. It says in Verse 33 "and he [the jailer] took them, Paul and Silas, [the prisoners], that very hour of the night and washed their wounds and immediately he, the jailer, was baptized - and all his household. And he brought them into his house and set food before them and rejoiced greatly having believed in God with his whole household." So here's another instantaneous conversion followed by baptism.

It's such an important point because if the Society were able to preach to prison guards in prisons or to the Governor of the prison, they would still tell them they have to get out of the government job. They must not serve the government because the governments are of the devil, so they wouldn't let him get baptized. Their whole approach can be shown to be very different to the attitude of the early Christians.

You might say, well what about the early church? The Society claimed that the early church was also neutral in time of war and would not violate their neutrality by joining the armed forces of Rome. But here's an interesting comment about that. It says, "What about the early church? Protestant historians have also noted the only two and possibly three church fathers (these church fathers were the leaders of the Christian church in the centuries immediately after the apostles, so that would be the second and third centuries) were openly opposed to participating in the military . The grounds of their rejection of military life are clearly seen to rest on the military's involvement with idolatry.

In addition, the military required an oath and certain garments of clothing and ceremonies and symbols, which were idolatrous in nature. As soon as those idolatrous circumstances were changed by Emperor Constantine, which happened in the early 4th Century, there no longer remained any reason why Christians should hesitate to be in the army. We find history shows that from the early 4th century on, more and more Christians agreed to go into the armed forces.

So it wasn't because of neutrality that these early Christians refused to get into the army; it was because the army practiced idolatry regularly every day and the Christians knew only too well that they must have absolutely nothing to do with that.

Does that mean, then, that Christians could be members of the armed service in times of war between nations? And the answer is a qualified "yes." Because you see it depends on whether it's an offensive war, an aggressive war, or a defensive war that you would be engaged in. For example in the Second World War, there was no question about who the aggressors were. It was Hitler and the Nazis and the armies of Germany. They were the aggressors because they started the whole thing. They started by invading Czechoslovakia. Then they took over Austria and attacked Poland. Britain and France had a non-aggression treaty with Poland, so, in order to honor their words and to defend the Polish people from the German attacks, Britain and France came to the defense of Poland. That's how World War II began.

It was considered righteous to be on the defensive against Hitler and his armies and personally speaking as a Christian, I completely agree with that. We may be able to look at later warfare like the war in Korea or maybe the war in Vietnam and say, "Well, we surely didn't have to get involved in that, did we?" It's debatable, and I don't intend to get into the details, but it's obvious when we think about this that it is possible under the right circumstances to fight a war on righteous terms.

I'd like to bring to your attention to an article that was written by Jehovah's Witnesses that appeared in their *Awake* magazine September the 8th, 1975. They're commenting on whether or not an individual could defend himself. Can you even defend yourself if you're a true Christian? This is what they had to say. "Jesus Christ did speak about turning the other cheek. At Matthew 5:39, He said "whoever slaps you on your right cheek, turn the other also to him." The Witnesses themselves comment on that and they say a slap is an insult often designed to provoke a fight. But by not retaliating when subjected to insulting speech or action, the Christian may prevent trouble, as it says in Proverbs 15 verse 1: "An answer when mild turns away rage." The situation, however, is very different when one is threatened with serious bodily harm. Now notice that that situation is different if instead of insulting you, your enemy is physically attacking you.

The Witnesses quote from Exodus 22:2: "If a thief should be found in the act of breaking into your house and he does get struck and die, there is no blood guilt on you." Then the Society comments "at night it would be very hard to determine the intentions of the intruder. To protect himself from possible harm, the homeowner had the right to inflict hard blows, and if these blows proved fatal, he was considered free from blood guilt."

The Watchtower Society is arguing that it's okay for individual Jehovah's Witnesses and their families to defend themselves in the event of their being brutally attacked with danger of inflicting bodily injury or harm on them. They're using Biblical scriptures to support that. They go on to say:

> "In view of increasing crime and violence, some Christians may wonder whether they should not arm themselves in preparation for possible attack. Jesus' apostles were known to have had at least two swords. That is not something unusual for the Jews at that time, because under the Mosaic Law, they allowed for armed conflict. Also swords were of value in warding off wild beasts and they could have served a utilitarian purpose."

So the thrust of this article which is on page 27 of the *Awake* magazine is to the effect, "Yeah, it's okay to defend yourselves providing the people who are attacking you are intent upon inflicting grievous bodily harm or death upon you and your family." We agree with that as Christians, but what's the difference in principle between protecting your family and protecting your country from its enemies? In principle there really isn't any difference to speak of. So I think the Watchtower Society has got things pretty much out of balance in this regard, and I think it's really important that Christians understand what the true situation is.

Now as a final comment on this particular subject, I I'll quote from a recent *Watchtower*, because it's one in which the Watchtower leaders change their view on this question of neutrality. They don't change it completely. They don't turn away from their idea that Christians have got to be neutral. The facts were if you claimed to be a conscientious objector then you would have to be examined by the authorities. You would have to appear at a meeting of local magistrates and be questioned about the position to see whether you were really sincerely a conscientious objector. What would happen is that the Witnesses of service age would be called in to see the magistrates (I'm thinking particularly of England because I was living there at the time) and the magistrates would ask the Witnesses to state their position and back it up scripturally if they could.

The Witnesses would do that. They would use the passages of Scripture I shared with you a little earlier on. When it was all over, the magistrates wouldn't argue with them. They would just ask them, would you be prepared to do alternative service? Instead of you going into the armed services, we'll let you go into some other occupation and serve in a non-aggressive kind of fashion. And the alternatives that the magistrates would give them would be, would you serve in the army as a member of the medical corps? And the Witnesses would say no, they wouldn't do that.

So they would ask, well, would you serve in a factory producing munitions? The Witnesses would say, no, we're definitely not going to do that. So lastly, they would say to them, would you serve as an orderly in hospital cleaning the floors? And they said, no, we're not going to do that either. When they said, no, we're not even going to clean floors in hospitals, then the magistrates would pass judgment on them and tell them, you are going to have to go to prison, and they would send them for a term in prison. So the Jehovah's Witnesses had to pay the price.

In 1996, just a few years ago, the Watchtower Society changed that. They talked about alternative service. "Civilian Service," this is the heading in the Watchtower. "However, there are lands where the state will not allow an exemption for ministers of religion, nevertheless acknowledges that some individuals may object to military service. Many of these lands make provisions for such conscientious individuals not to be forced into military service.

In some places, required civilian service, such as useful work in the community is regarded as a non-military national service. Could an educated Christian undertake such service? Here again, a dedicated baptized Christian would have to make his own decision on the basis of his Bible-trained conscious. See, it's saying now each individual Witness can now make up their own mind, and if they feel that serving in the civilian community in some capacity is not the same as military service, then they can go for it.

In the article I wrote at the time, I said this change in teaching would undoubtedly make life easier for thousands of young Jehovah's Witness men in many countries if and when war breaks out. But what about those who suffered for nothing? And don't forget, by reversing its teaching, the Society tacitly admits its original ruling was false. So were all those sacrifices made by so many people just an example of religiously duped people laboring in vain? That's really what it was. The Society, with all its authority had made that decision on behalf of the rank and file members and they all followed suit slavishly. A lot of those young men suffered terribly during those war years, and some of them died. Some of them were assassinated or executed. Many of them were tortured, and now it turns out that it was all for nothing. It was all unnecessary. They could have taken an alternative in the first place. Isn't that something?

A final comment has to be made on this subject because it reveals, I think, more clearly than anything else how mistaken the Society is in its attempt to interpret the Bible. It has to do with this subject of neutrality. It's Roman's chapter 13, starting at verse I. It says:

> Let every person be in subjection to the governing
> authorities, for there is no authority except from God,
> and those which exist are established by God. Therefore,
> he who resists authority has opposed the ordinance of God
> and they who have opposed will receive condemnation upon
> themselves. For rulers is not a cause of fear for good be-
> havior but for evil. Do you want to have no fear of author-
> ity? Do what is good, and you will have praise from the
> same, for it is a minister of God to you for your good; but
> if you do what is evil, be afraid, for it does not bear the
> sword for nothing, for it is a minister of God, an avenger,
> who bring wrath upon the one who practices evil.

Here's the interesting thing about that. The apostle
Paul in his letter to the Roman Church is advising Christians that they have got to be in subjection to the governing
authorities. There is no question about it. The early readers of the Watchtower under a man named Pastor Russell,
the first president of the Watchtower, accepted that. They
believed it and they interpreted it in the same way that
most of the Protestant churches interpret it, that the "rulers" were the rulers of this world - government leaders and
kings, etc.

But along comes the second leader of the Watchtower
Society, Judge Rutherford, and he completely changes the
interpretation. He says the authorities referred to in Romans 13 are no less than Jehovah God and his son, Christ
Jesus! So he was able to change the whole approach of
Jehovah's Witnesses to this subject. We're not in subjection
to the kings and the government rulers or anything like
that. We're only in subjection to God and Jesus.

The trouble is, and it's very obvious, that the Bible is
saying it's the secular government that is a minister of God,
because it talks about (verse 4) not doing evil, for "it," that's
the secular government or authority, is a minister of God
to you for good. Least you do what is evil be afraid, for it
doesn't bear the sword for nothing. It's a minister of God
who brings wrath upon the one who practices evil."

The idea is if you're a crook, and if you're habitually a lawbreaker and steal and do all sorts of criminal activities, then the government is like a minister of God. It's a minister on God's behalf to exact punishment and to judge you. That's the whole idea of the passage. It goes on to say, "for because of this, you also pay taxes, for rulers are servants of God devoting themselves to this very thing." Well, those taxes are paid to secular rulers. The Jews at the time were paying a tax to Rome as well as a tax to their own Sanhedrin and leaders, so the Watchtower made a total mess of this.

Their reason for doing that was because they believed at that time that the whole world was directly under the power of Satan the devil, and that Satan was the one responsible for raising up all the governments. The Society held to this false teaching from approximately 1930-1960. It didn't matter what country you lived in, your government had been put there by the devil. But in reality, Romans 13 says it's God that raised up those governments and established them. It says in verses 1-2:

> For there is no authority except from God and those which exist are established by God; therefore he who resists authority has opposed the ordinance of God; and they who have opposed will receive condemnation upon themselves.

It's true that Satan can and does influence government members to do evil, because even government members are sinful humans and can sin. Nevertheless, the Holy Bible insists that God is in charge. He raises up and installs these human governments. Governments have been authorized to rule by God Himself. Daniel 5:21 says, "... the Most High God is ruler over the realm of mankind and that He sets over It whom He wishes."

For Christians, this means we must obey our human rulers - the only exception being rules by human governments that contradict God's clearly stated Biblical rules (see Matthew 22:15-21; Acts 5:29).

Chapter 13

The Deity of Christ

The Christian position is that the Holy Bible teaches that God is Triune; a being composed of three Divine spirit persons. One of whom we identify as God the Father, the other One whom we identify as the Son of God, and the third One we identify as the Holy Spirit.

The Society has a serious misconception of the Trinity. It's amazing their misconception of what is taught by the Christian churches on the doctrine of the Trinity.

In one of their magazines they make a brief statement about the doctrine of the Trinity on how the churches view the trinity and they actually get it right.. In the June 15th 1987 edition it just simply says,

> "But what exactly is the Trinity? The Waverly encyclopedia defines it as the mystery as one God in three persons; the Father, the Son, and the Holy Ghost, coequal and coeternal in all things."

That's a very brief definition but it is adequate, it covers the point. The amazing thing is that if we look at the Watchtower publications that have been produced over the years, since the early days of the Watchtower Society, we'll see that they have been incredibly confused about this doctrine. I'd like to examine a number of quotations on this topic from Watchtower leaders going back to the late nineteen hundreds, in the days when Pastor Russell was the primary teacher of the organization. I want you to just follow this line of argument with me and let's see if we can get the point.

The first reference is a quotation from the nineteen hundred and six publication call *The Atonement*. It's part of the series that Russell produced called, *Studies in the Scriptures*. From volume five, page 55 of that book he said this:

> "HKingdomd there be three Gods and yet only one God?"

Do you see the mistake there? The Trinity doctrine does not consist in the idea that there are three Gods in one, or three Gods in anything. There is how many Gods? One God composed of three Divine persons. Here we are back in the early years of the Watchtower organization and they are putting forward the idea that the Trinity doctrine is three Gods in One God.

A second reference comes from the nineteen twenty-eight publication called, *Reconciliation*. This publication was produced by the second leader of the Watchtower, Judge Rutherford. Under the heading *Trinity* we find this:

> The doctrine taught by the clergymen and which since have been followed by others, which in brief is that there are three Gods in one, God the Father, God the Son, and God the Holy Ghost.

There again you see coming from nineteen hundred and six to nineteen twenty-nine this concept of three Gods in one.

Interestingly enough, in the previous year, nineteen twenty-eight, the Watchtower December first issue made this statement in reference to 1 John 5:7:

> The Trinity doctrine assumes that three distinct persons are mentioned in this text. The idea that three separate and distinct persons can be One person, is unreasonable, unscriptural, and utterly impossible.

Did you get that point? They are now talking about the idea of there being three persons in one person! Now none of these assertions corresponds with the Christian doctrine of the Triune nature of God or the Trinity. These are totally wrong concepts. We see they go backwards and forwards in their publications on trying to define what the Trinity is all about.

The *Watchtower* of April 1, 1970 speaks about the name Jehovah:

> If he is one Jehovah then could he be three Gods, God the Father, God the Son, and the Holy Ghost as the Trinitarians teach? Let God answer. No, Jehovah could not be three Gods for the Bible plainly says that He is One God.

Isn't this amazing, this flip flop backwards and forwards between continually giving wrong definitions of what the Trinity is all about.

Almost 10 years later in the July 1st, 1979 edition of the *Watchtower* we read:

> But we totally reject as unscriptural the teaching that Jehovah, Jesus and God's Spirit or active force are three Gods in one person.

Well that's a switch isn't it? That's the third definition. Three Gods in one, three persons in one person, and now we've got three Gods in one person.

We have to say in all honesty, that the leaders of the Jehovah Witnesses have reveled through their publications that they are extremely confused and lacking in knowledge about what the Trinity doctrine really represents.

On page 39 of the Witness's book *You Can Live Forever in Paradise on Earth*, published in 1982, it says:

> Since Jesus prayed to God asking that God's will not His be done, the two could not be the same person.

Isn't it incredible, the confusion that exits among the leaders of the Watchtower. They certainly are unable to direct the witnesses in what the Trinity is really all about.

What about that question that Jesus prayed to Himself? How could that be? Well, I think you should already have a clue. If the God of the Bible is composed of three Divine spirit persons, and one of those persons, His center of intelligence and personality, is located here on the earth for awhile and takes up residence in the body and the human nature of Jesus; then one of the persons of God on earth could surely communicate in prayer to the other person of God in Heaven. Wouldn't that be true? It couldn't be too difficult for that to take place. So the idea that when Jesus engaged in prayer to the Father He was praying to Himself is just nonsense. Jesus was praying to the Person of God the Father in Heaven.

Now I think it's good to remember what Jesus had to do in order to become a man on earth. Let's turn to Philippians 2:5-7, and take a look at this to see if it helps to throw some light on this situation. It says:

> Have this attitude in yourselves which was also in Christ Jesus, who, although He existed in the form of God, did not regard equality with God a thing to be grasped, but emptied Himself, taking the form of a bond-servant, and being made in the likeness of men.

For that to happen God really would have to put His divine prerogatives into the background for awhile. And if I could use the very mundane expression, the divine nature of God in Jesus would have to take a backseat while the human nature of Jesus would grow, develop, and flourish as a human nature should. You can well appreciate that if the Divine nature that was resident in Christ was continually manifesting itself in all the glory, magnificence and splendor of the Almighty infinite God, then it's obvious that the human nature of Jesus would be totally overwhelmed. For that matter, all humans around Him would be overwhelmed as well.

The Divine nature was suppressed while Christ was on the earth in order for His human nature to function. We see all kinds of things happening that we would expect to happen if Jesus were really a man. Mainly as John chapter 4 said; He was tired after the long journey and He became hungry. God Himself, the divine nature, neither gets tired nor gets hungry.

Jesus also prayed. In fact, as a perfect man without sin, He would be the role model for all humans to follow. All humans, that is, who believe in God. Jesus would demonstrate throughout His life what it means for a person to function properly as a human, and the correct relationship that they should have to God the Father in Heaven.

Prayer of course, is the very essential part of our relationship with God, do you not agree? Jesus, by continual prayer, was certainly demonstrating that for us.

Here are the two reasons put forward by Jehovah Witnesses as to why they insist that Jesus cannot be God. They say he cannot be God because Jesus Himself was created, He had a beginning. Obviously, God by definition is uncreated and never had a beginning. The second reason they would argue that Jesus cannot be God, is because Jesus is revealed in Scripture as not being equal to God. Almighty God could hardly be inferior to Himself, now could He? If they can make a case on those two points, then we would have to accept that their position is correct.

We are going to take a look in detail at some of the primary passages of Scripture that the Witnesses use in order to support those two contentions.

Beginning with argument number one: Jesus was created. The primary passages of Scripture they use are found in Proverbs 8:22, Colossians 1:16, and Revelation 3:14. We'll examine each in turn. By the way, I'm going to quote from the Watchtower Bible, because they have changed it a little.

Proverbs 8:22 in context is talking about the wisdom of God. It is true that the writer of Proverbs takes this quality of wisdom and personifies that quality and writes in such a way as if wisdom were a person or had personality. Because of that the Jehovah Witnesses say, it must describing

Jesus in His prehuman condition. You see the idea? Verse twenty-two from the Witnesses *New World Translation* reads:

> Jehovah himself produced me as the beginning of his way the earliest of his achievements of long ago.

Did you notice the difference between their Bible and yours? Doesn't your Bible say, The Lord Himself possessed me? Well to possess something and to produce something are two different things. The concept of producing something means to bring it into existence. This is the idea that the Watchtower is trying to create that Jesus is the wisdom of God and was brought into existence.

But listen, the wisdom of God is an attribute of God, is it not? God is from everlasting. He is eternal. He has always been God. Can you imagine there actually existed a time when the Almighty God of the universe had no quality of wisdom? Can you imagine that? And if He didn't have wisdom at one time, where on earth did he get if from? Obviously the correct translation should be, the Lord "possessed" me, not produced me. They also try to use verse thirty from the same chapter. Wisdom is still speaking as a person:

> I came to be beside Him, [that's beside God] as a master worker and I came to be the one He was specially fond of day by day, I being glad before Him all the time.

From this they say that Jesus here is personified as wisdom, created or produced by God like a master worker, working at the side of Jehovah in His other works of creation.

I would suggest to you that this passage in Proverbs eight has no relationship to Jesus at all. It's not talking about Christ in His prehuman condition. One of the reasons I would say that is because what it says in your Bible, Quoting from the New American Standard Bible:

> Does not wisdom call, And understanding lift up her voice? On top of the heights beside the way, Where the paths meet, she takes her stand; Beside the gates, at the opening to the city, At the entrance of the doors, she cries out: (Proverbs 8:1-3)

What do you notice about wisdom? Feminine. Wisdom is personified all right but wisdom is personified as a woman, not as a man. I'm going to suggest to you that there is no way, and I hope you are not going to accuse me of male chauvinism here, that Jesus the Son of God is going to be depicted in anyway in the Old Testament Scriptures under the figure of a woman. Is that okay?

Now the leaders of Jehovah Witnesses didn't like the feminine gender, so would you believe, they changed it. Let me read Proverbs eight verse 1 and 2 in their Bible.

> Does not wisdom keep calling out and discernment keep giving forth it's voice? On the top of the heights by the way at the crossing of the roadways it has stationed itself.

They have taken the feminine gender and changed it deliberately into the neuter gender. Unfortunately, very often the leadership of the Watchtower has this situation where the left hand doesn't know what the right hand is doing. In 1974 they published a little book called *God's Eternal Purpose Now Triumphing*. On page 28 they actually admitted that Proverbs eight is in the feminine gender:

> This reminds us of what he said in the eighth chapter of the book of Proverbs where divine wisdom is pictured as a person who talks about himself. Of course in the original Hebrew text of Proverbs the word wisdom is in the feminine and speaks of itself as a female person.

That's clear enough isn't it? And without any explanation at all they just calmly make there Bible read in the neuter gender. These little points are worth bringing to the attention as you try to witness to them.

Proverbs eight then, does not support their idea that Jesus was created in Heaven and that Jesus had a beginning before He came to the earth. Let's move to Colossians 1:13. You'll notice it's talking about God's beloved Son. In verse 15 it says He is the image of the invisible God the firstborn of all creation.

Now what do you think Jehovah Witnesses do with that? Notice the expression firstborn of all creation? They'll say, look there it is. It says it right there in the Bible, in black and white. The Son of God Jesus, was the first thing that God ever created. My friends that is not what that verse says. Now please notice the expression very carefully that Jesus, the Son of God, is "the firstborn" of all creation. Now what does that word mean? The word "firstborn" in the Greek language is not the same as "first created." They are two different expressions. There is a word in the Greek language that means first created but the Apostle Paul didn't choose that he chose the Greek word for firstborn, "Prototokos." Now if we do a word study on the use of that word throughout the Bible we would discover that it is used in two ways only. The first way is the obvious way referring to the firstborn child in a family, that's clear enough. The second way is that it's used as a title, a title indicating pre-eminence over all other things. It's in that sense that firstborn is being used by the Apostle Paul. A good cross reference to establish this kind of use of the word firstborn is in Psalm 89.

Let's look at Psalm 89 and what it says. We'll find that God is talking about King David, who was one of the great Israelite Kings. If you look at Psalm 89 verse 20 God says,

I have found David my servant with My holy oil I have anointed him.

So we are definitely talking about King David. Now look at verse 27. God says,

"I also shall make him My firstborn the highest of the Kings of the earth."

It should be pretty obvious if you know the background and history of David and his family that he was by no means the first of Jesse's sons. Jesse had at least seven other sons before he had David. David was in no sense a literal first-born, but you notice that God says quite clearly, "I'm going to make David My firstborn." Now how is He going to do that? He's not going to send David back into his mother's womb is He, and have him born as the first member of the family? Of course not. It's a title, and the indication is in the end of verse 27:

> ,,,I'm going to make him the highest of the kings of the earth.

The same principle applies here in Colossians 1:15 concerning Jesus. He is called, firstborn of all creation, because He has preeminence over all created things.

How can we be sure that's correct and that it is not talking about the fact that Jesus Himself was created up there in Heaven by Jehovah? Let's look at verse 16:

> For by Him [Jesus] all things were created both in the Heavens and on the earth, visible or invisible; whether they're thrones or dominions, or rulers, or authorities: all things have been created by Him and for Him.

That's pretty clear isn't it? This is absolutely clear that the Son of God is identified as the creator of every single thing in the Heavens and of the earth. It doesn't matter whether they are visible or whether they are invisible things, the Son of God created everything.

Of course, that's such a powerful verse of Scripture that the Watchtower had to change it

In Colossians chapter 1 verse 16 in their Bible, it says:

> Because by means of him all other things were created in the heavens upon the earth, the things visible and the things invisible no matter whether they're thrones, lordships, government, or authorities, all other things have been created through him and for him.

I would suggest my dear friends that that's dishonest. Wouldn't you? The Witnesses have a reference Bible they call the *Kingdom Interlinear* Bible, which is the New Testament along with the Greek text and the literal English words underneath. They put their translation in the right hand column. If you discuss this topic with the Witnesses, get them to look it up in that Bible. Make them look across on the left hand side to the Greek words and the literal English words, you'll see there is no word "other" in that text whatsoever.

Let's look at Revelation 3:14. This is another of their favorite verses. It says,

> And to the angel of the church in Laodicea write; The Amen, the faithful and true Witness, the Beginning of the creation of God, says this:

Notice that Jesus is giving Himself the titles of the Amen, the Faithful, and true Witness, and He also calls Himself "the Beginning of creation of God."

Can you see what the Witnesses would do with that? Jesus is the first thing God created, He's the beginning of God's creation. My dear friend that's not what it means.

The word beginning is wider in its application then we might think it is. Usually when we use the word beginning we mean the start of something, or the first part of something. If I say to you I am going to Los Angeles at the beginning of next week, you expect me to go there in the first part of the week. That is generally how we use the word beginning.

But in actual fact, if you look the word up in a dictionary, you'll find that we use the beginning to indicate a source or origin of something. It is that sense in which John is using it in the book of Revelation. He is saying that Jesus, the Amen, is also the source of all God's creation.

A good cross-reference to compare here is Revelation 21:6-7. Almighty God is speaking to John the Apostle:

> And he said unto me, It is done. I am Alpha and
> Omega, the beginning and the end. I will give unto him
> that is athirst of the fountain of the water of life freely. He
> that overcometh shall inherit all things; and I will be his
> God, and he shall be my son.

Now if you ask Jehovah Witnesses who speaking here, who is it that's calling Himself the Alpha and the Omega. The Witnesses will tell you right away, Oh that's Jehovah, Almighty God. So you say to them, doesn't the Alpha and Omega say, I am the beginning. Doesn't it say that? Yes, God says I am the Alpha and the Omega the beginning and the end. Now if God is the beginning does that mean He is the first part of His own creation? He was the first thing that was created. Of course not. We know God is from everlasting. But we also know that God is the source or origin of all creation. Do we not know that? Therefore the word beginning means source or origin.

Do you realize something? We have taken the best three pet verses of the Jehovah Witnesses and proven they do not support the concept that Jesus was created or had a beginning. See the point?

I will tell you an interesting thing about this, the psychology of this. If you had a conversation with the Witnesses about Jesus, and they come on to you about this business that Jesus was created, you can say to them, "Hey that's interesting. You say Jesus was created, does the Bible really teach that." They'll say yes and probably quote one of the verses, say Colossians 1:15. Then as a matter of interest you could say to them, "How many verses are there in the Bible that tell us that Jesus was created?" You would be amazed at the answers you get. It would vary from dozens, to the Bible is full of them. NO it isn't! The Witnesses only have those three verses and they keep appealing to them over and over again in their publications. It's always the same three passages; Proverbs 8, Colossians 1, and Revelations 3.

Actually, we have just shown that they don't have a leg to stand on. There is no statement in the Holy Bible to the effect that Jesus was created before He came to this earth, or that He had a beginning up there in Heaven.

Let's proceed to our next argument. Remember the Society teaches that Jesus is not equal to God, but inferior to God. Now if they could prove that they would have a very strong point.

Lets look at John 14:28. Here's a well known statement where Jesus says:

> "You heard that I said to you, 'I go away, and I will come to you.' If you loved Me, you would have rejoiced, because I go to the Father; for the Father is greater than I."

The Witnesses really like that verse and use it frequently. They clKingdomt verse proves that Jesus is not equal to God the Father. Jesus says in that verse that the Father is greater than I. He says it plain as anything. Now what can we say in reply to that.

This is a good example of how people like Jehovah Witnesses can fail to understand how words can be used in the Holy Scriptures.

Let me make a statement to you to throw a little light on it. Suppose I said to you, "Greater is not better." Would you agree? In the Greek language they are two different words just as they are in the English. Greater is not better. Let me explain. The President of the United States is greater than I am, but he is not better than I am. What makes the President of the United States greater than I? His office. He occupies the office or position of the supreme political head of the most powerful government in the world, and I don't. I'm just a humble teacher of the Word. Why is it that the President of the United States is not better than I? The answer is because he's human and I'm human. He has all the identifying qualities of humanity. He's not an angel, he's not God, just a fellow human. Would you agree? He posseses human nature and I posses human nature. The President may be greater than me as to his office, but we are perfectly equal when it comes to sharing the human nature. The same thing applies to the two persons of God we're talking about, the Father, and the Son.

The Father remained in Heaven in overall supervision of everything going on this earth and in the universe, while the Son humbled Himself and came to this earth to be a man and perform a very humble role on earth. Positionally the Father was greater because He occupied the supreme office, while the Son emptied Himself to be a man. At the same time the Father was not better than the Son, because they both shared the same God nature, the same unique nature of God. Are you with me? This verse does not prove Jesus is less than God.

John 20:17 is another favorite of the Witnesses which opens a whole new area of thinking. This is after Christ rose from the dead and met Mary in the garden. It is here she attempts to hold on to Him. Jesus responds by saying to her,

> "...Stop clinging to Me, for I've not yet ascended to the Father; but go to My brethren,..."

I want you to notice the message that Jesus gives Mary to take to the Disciples. Please notice that He calls them brothers. He says, "You go to My brethren and you say to them I ascend to My Father and your Father and My God and your God." How about that one? Witnesses will say, look, here's the resurrected Jesus still talking about somebody up there in Heaven, that's His God. So how could Jesus possibly be God? Does God call God, God?

The answer is, YES He does! Try looking at Hebrews 1:8 sometime and you'll see what I mean, God the Father calls the Son, God. This is a very important part of Christian theology that you don't hear too much. When Jesus rose from the dead, it was His human body and His human nature that rose from the dead; the Divine nature never died anyway. Are you with me? Because the Divine nature of God cannot die.

When the human nature rose from the dead, Jesus was a resurrected man. When He ascended back to Heaven He became a glorified man. The Divine nature was now residing in a human body and a human nature that has been glorified. Jesus is here establishing that great truth to His disciples and that's why He didn't say to Mary, go and tell my disciples, He said go and tell my brothers. He was trying to convey the humanity brotherhood concept, which was very real for them. He said, "I'm ascending to My Father and He's your Father too." Which was true wasn't it? Because they were becoming sons of God. He said I'm ascending to My God and your God. The relationship between the humanity of Jesus and the Divine nature is the relationship of a human to his God. That is why Jesus could speak that way.

We see in a most remarkable fashion how the Bible writers portray Jesus like the two sides of a coin. They are continually presenting His human face to us and then as it were a few verses latter turning the coin over and presenting His Divine nature to us. This theme runs all the way through the New Testament Scriptures.

The next passages are in 1 Corinthians. The first one comes up in chapter 8 verse 6. It is quite a complex passage of Scripture. The Apostle Paul is talking to Christians:

> For us there is but One God the Father from whom
> all things are, and we exist for Him, and One Lord Jesus
> Christ by whom all things are, and we exist through Him.

Can imagine what the Society can do with that verse? You see, they say it tells you there is to the Christians but one God, and who is that? The Father! See that?

It's all over now, it's an open and shut case, we might as well close our Bibles up and go home, right? Not so quick. We have to understand why Paul talks about the Father being God, and why he talks about Jesus being Lord.

Let's back up a bit and look at the surrounding verses and we'll discover that what the Apostle is doing is, contrasting the polytheistic many god worship of the pagans, with the monotheistic one God worship of Christians.

Beginning with verse four the Apostle Paul says:

> Concerning eating the things sacrificed to idols we know there is no such thing as an idol in the world and there is no God but One. For even if there are so called gods whether in Heaven or on earth, as indeed there are many gods and many lords yet for us there is but one God the Father and one Lord Jesus Christ.

He is very clear there's no god but One. He's back to the theme of the One true God. But then in verse five he starts to talk about the deities or the objects of worship of the nations. He says there are so called gods, whether in Heaven or in earth, as indeed there are many gods and many lords. If we look back over history we'll see that the pagan deities or gods were conceived of both being heavenly and earthly. In fact, aren't the planets of our solar system named after some of their ancient gods. Mars, for instance, is the god of war. Venus, represents the goddess of love, and so on. There are earthly gods as well. Pharaoh of Egypt was worshiped as a god and so was Ceasar of Rome. Up until the end of World War II, Emperor Hirohito of Japan, was worshiped by the Japanese as a god. The pagan nations did have their heavenly and earthly gods.

Notice what the Apostle does now in verse five, he says,

> For even if there are so-called gods, whether in heaven or on earth (as indeed there are many "gods" and many "lords")

That's what he's saying. What are these pagan deities? They are gods plural and lords plural. And he's showing that they were the two terms that the pagan peoples would use to describe their deities. They would call them god or they would call them lord, and they had many of them.

But now in contrast the Christian only has one deity whom he addresses as God or Lord. He addresses that deity as God in the form of the Father, and Lord in the form of Jesus.

Now if these two terms were mutually exclusive terms then we would have to be able to say to the Jehovah Witnesses, okay, now there is only one God and that's the Father. And how many lords are there for the Christian? The Witness would have to say there is only one Lord. Then you would say, "Who's that?" Jesus Christ. Therefore you are telling me that if you can only call the Father God by the same argument you can only call Jesus Lord. How does it come about that even in your Bible God the Father, Jehovah, is also called Lord; and how does it come about in your Bible that Jesus the Lord is also called God. Isn't this true? Yes. And if you don't think that Jehovah in the Watchtower Bible is ever called Lord just take a look at Acts 17:24 sometime and take a look at Revelation 11:15. You will see in the Watchtower Bible, the *New World Translation*, how the sovereign creator of the universe is called Lord by the Christians. Can you think of any verse in the Bible where Jesus is called God? Of course. Matthew 1:23, Emmanuel, which translated means God with us. John 1:1, the Word was God. John 20:28, Thomas says to Jesus my Lord and my God. Thomas uses both titles together. We have to understand that this verse here in 1 Corinthians chapter 8 is not using mutually exclusive terms, both the word god and the word lord are used by pagans to identify their deities and by Christians to identify their One deity.

Now let's go to chapter 11 in 1 Corinthians, verse 3. Here we have the principle of headship and the balancing principle of subjection. Verse 3 says to the Christians,

> I want you to understand that Christ is the head of
> every man, and the man is the head of the woman and
> God is the head of Christ.

The Witnesses will point out that it says that God is
the head of Christ, so Jesus is less than God and therefore
He cannot be God.

I'm afraid they've misunderstood the principle of
headship and also the principle of subjection. Jesus was
determined to be subordinate to the Father. Back in the
days of eternity all three persons of the triune God coun-
selled together, (according to Ephesians chapter one), and
made all the decisions about creation and salvation. The
Son of God was the one who took on the task of coming to
the earth and carrying out the work of redemption for us.

The position of headship and subjection does not interfere with Christ's equality with His Father at all. Look
at the middle section of verse three where it says, "The man
is the head of the woman." You married ladies let me ask
you a question. Is your husband therefore superior to you,
and you are inferior to your husband? Isn't that right? Did I
hear a no? Let me tell you something, if I had a meeting
place full of Jehovah Witnesses ladies they would also say
no. They would probably say it even more loudly then you
did. No, oh no! Just because God has designated my husband to be my head doesn't make him a superior form of life
to me, he's only human as I am human. Quite right ladies.
It's an arrangement of headship and subjection for the purpose of good order and getting things done. That principle
applies whenever you have intelligent persons working together on any work or scheme or plan or project. Don't you
have the principle of headship in the Armed Forces? Don't
you have the principle of headship in companies and the
boards of directors? You have the principle of headship in
families and so on. But in no way does it detract from the
essential quality of nature. If you could take a board of directors in a company today, and John Smith is elected chairman of the board; Can you imagine him as he sticks his

thumbs behind his suspenders and goes waltzing around
the offices saying goodie, goodie, I am a superior form of
life to all you other people. I don't think he would be chairman of the board very long.

Just as John Smith has the office, function, and position of chairman, so is the position and the function of the
Father within the plans and purposes of God. The position
and function of the Son is to be subordinate to the Father in
this great work of salvation. The Holy Spirit as well has a
position and function. He is to be in subjection to both the
Father and the Son, because the Bible says the Father sends
the Holy Spirit and the Bible says the Son sends the Holy
Spirit. The Bible never says the Holy Spirit sends either
the Father or the Son. Is that not true?

So we have to understand these Bible principles not
interfering in any way in the essential equality of nature
that Jesus the Son of God shares with His Father, thus identifying Him as the true God.

There is one final line of argument raised by the Witnesses that I want to deal with which is based upon John
1:18:

> No man has seen God at any time, the only begotten
> God that is in the bosom of the Father has explained Him.

The Witnesses will use this verse and insist the Bible
says no man has ever seen God. They'll claim further, they
saw Jesus didn't they? For years He walked around the village of Nazareth and went back to Jerusalem and stood on
the mountain side and taught the people. He wasn't invisible. They could see Him. So how come they could see Jesus,
and yet the Bible says that no man has seen God? Yet you
want me to believe that Jesus is God.

They think they have caught you in something that is
totally self-contradictory. Listen, what does the Bible mean
when it says no man has seen God? Did you know that there
are passages in the Old Testament where the faithful servants of God in the Old Testament claim to have seen God?

Isaiah 6:1-5, the profit Isaiah says, "Woe is me I'm undone I'm a man of unclean lips dwelling in a land of unclean people and yet mine eyes have seen the Lord the King of hosts." Isaiah didn't die, God didn't crush Isaiah out of existence and yet the Old Testament says that no man can see God and live. What was it that Isaiah really saw? He saw a vision of God, he saw God in visionary form. He couldn't see God in God's essential Glory.

In Judges 13:15-23 we've an interesting case of a faithful servant of God, an Israelite man by the name of Manoah. He and his wife are visited by the angel of the Lord. They also have a conversation with the angel of the Lord. Verse 21 says:

> Now the angel of the Lord who had been appearing to them, appeared no more to Manoah or his wife. Then Manoah knew that He was the angel of the Lord. So Manoah said to his wife we shall surely die for we have seen God.

Doesn't it say that? Please notice that his wife didn't contradict him she just said; look if the Lord had desired to kill us He would not have accepted our burnt offering but He did. Thus equating the angel of the Lord with the Almighty God Himself. What had happened was that God Himself, or one of the persons of God had visited Manoah and his wife and spoken to them, as a man or an angel. You could never see God in all His Glory because God is light, and the Glory of God is so enormous that you could no more get close to God then you could get to the sun of our solar system.

Hebrew 12:29 says, "Our God is also a consuming fire." Therefore when people looked at Jesus they didn't see the Divine nature in Him blazing out in glory because it was on the backburner, all they could see was a man.

But nevertheless, Jesus said in John 14 to Philip, "He that has seen Me has seen the Father." Don't let the Witnesses get away with any their arguments that they use to try and prove that Jesus could not be God.

Answering Questions Christians Raise

Question: You've mentioned their Interlinear Bible. I've been kind of curious, can I get a hold of this?

Answer: Well, they are becoming more and more difficult to get but I would recommend that you write directly to the Watchtower headquarters in Brooklyn, I think the price of the Interlinear is about $4.50. If you sent them a check for $6.00 and requested a copy, I think they would probably send it to you through the mail. Their address is available on the internet.

Question: I'm looking at a Sept 15, 1910 issue of Watchtower, and I know that they despise the cross. But on their logo here on top they have two pictures of the cross. How do they explain that?

Answer: They'll say that's a good example of new light. They'll claim the light of truth gets brighter and brighter as the day draws near and quote Proverbs 4:18. They'll say, yes there was a time when we've believed in all those false Babylonish symbols, but we've become enlightened since then. But what happened was that Judge Rutherford, after he took over following the death of Pastor Russell, was looking for some ways in which he could make the Jehovah Witnesses appear to be completely different from all the other religions around. So he chose the cross and said that was a pagan symbol and the Bible doesn't say that Jesus died on a cross. That's why he did it.

Incidentally, I'd like to add there is plenty of evidence, both archaeological and scriptural to indicate that Jesus did die on the cross.

Question: I was wondering in Hebrews 1:8, if it reads the same way in the Jehovah Witnesses Bible as it does in our Bible?

Answer: Hebrews 1:8 is one of those verse where I said we have God calling God, God. First from the New American Standard Bible, "But of the Son He [that's a reference to God] says Thy throne O God is forever and ever." You see that? Here's God the Father speaking to God the Son and calling Him God; "Thy throne O God is forever." Well of course that didn't sit very well with the Jehovah Witnesses, so guess what they did?

They changed it! Here's how it reads in their Bible:

> But with reference to the Son, God is your throne forever and ever.

See the difference? You may ask, what on earth could that possibly mean? Think about it. He's addressing the Son and He says, "God is your throne." Could it mean that when Jesus went up into Heaven He sat down on God. It's a foolish statement. Yet so determined are they to get rid of all the evidence of Christ's Godship and deity, that they would do a foolish thing like that.

Question: I am curious about Colossians 1:16 as a response to their tendency to use Colossians 1:15. I noticed in Dr. Martin's tape with Bill Cetnar, the former Jehovah Witness, he uses that as a response. Have you had any encounters yourself in Christians witnessing. Is it really effective with Jehovah Witnesses?

Answer: It can be effective, but it depends how clearly you examine it with him. A good thing to do to make it really effective, is to get him to compare Colossians 1:16 with John 1:3, in his Bible. There is a close parallel between the two. In John it reveals that all things come into existence from the Word, "All things came into existence through Him and apart from Him not even one thing came into existence."

Question: In Luke chapter 5, and Mark chapter 2, Jesus heals the paralytic and then forgives his sins. The Pharisees reply, "Who can forgive sins but God alone?" I'd like to know how the Society treats these two accounts.

Answer: They would try to say its true, only God can forgive sins, but God delegated that authority to Jesus. He conferred that authority on Him. Then they'll say it's rather similar to the way Jesus delegated authority to His disciples in John 20:23 where He said, "If you forgive somebody sins then their sins are forgiven and if do not forgive then their sins are not forgiven." Authority conferred to the disciples. What the Witnesses don't realize is the different meaning behind the two situations. Jesus never said anywhere in any of the gospels that God had given Him the authority to forgive sins. In one case He says He has the authority to judge but never does it say He had the authority given Him to forgive sins, this was assumed by Him to be His natural prerogative. Now in contrast, when Jesus said to His disciples in John 20, "Whoever sins you forgive will be forgiven and whose ever sins you hold they will not be forgiven." We do not find any of the disciples then going out saying to people, child your sins are forgiven. They never did that. All they did was use the authority they had been given and preached the gospel. People's sins were forgiven, or withheld from forgiveness, on the basis on how they reacted to the gospel message preached by the Apostle.

Question: God says that you are not supposed to change or add to His word. It's obvious that the Jehovah Witnesses are really changing the Bible. How do they justify that? What can I say if I am approached by a Jehovah's Witness?

Answer: They would claim that they are not really changing the Bible. They are changing it back to what it really meant. In other words, they are changing it back to the original. One of their most serious changes is John 8:58 where Jesus called Himself I AM. Another would be Acts 20:20. You might want to make a note of these and use them as glaring examples. Be sure to use the *Kingdom Interlinear Bible*.

Question: How do the Jehovah Witnesses explain John 10:33, where Jesus says I and My Father are One. The Jews then attempt to stone Him for claiming to be God.

Answer: The Witnesses do have a way to try to get around it. Look carefully at John 10:33-36.

> The Jews answered Him, "For a good work we do not stone You, but for blasphemy; and because You, being a man, make Yourself out to be God." Jesus answered them,

"Has it not been written in your Law, "I SAID, YOU ARE GODS'? "If he called them gods, to whom the word of God came (and the Scripture cannot be broken), do you say of Him, whom the Father sanctified and sent into the world, "You are blaspheming,' because I said, "I am the Son of God'?

The Witnesses will say Jesus is saying that the Bible is talking about other people being gods, so what's the big deal about Jesus claiming to be a god.

We need to understand why certain people were called Gods in the Old Testament, because Jesus was quoting Psalm 82 where humans were called gods. In Psalm 82 God is speaking to the rulers and judges of Israel. He is condemning them because they have perverted justice and shown themselves to be gross sinners. They've defrauded the widow and the orphan and things like this. God is therefore chastising them when He says, "I say you are gods but you will die like men." God is speaking as it were sarcastically. You see? Oh, you're gods are you; you think yourself gods but you're going to die like men. We can see the gods of Psalm 82 are not true gods at all, but are really false gods aren't they?

Question: Will Witnesses deny their doctrines when cornered?

Answered: That's a good question. The tendency is to want to deny the problem and remain loyal to the leadership. These are all natural human tendencies. You on the other hand must be very clear in the information you present so there can be no misunderstanding their belief is in error. Additionally, you should be very sincere in your motives. The Witness must see from observing you that you're not just interested in putting him down, or breaking down their loyalty to leaders; you are genuinely concerned about his eternal destiny. If they sense this from you, then they are going to be far more likely to accept what you tell them, even though it pains them and hurts them to do so. The sincerity and the conviction you have when addressing them is of the utmost importance.

That was the thing that effected me when I would occasionally meet a Christian who would share with me. It wasn't just what they said, it was the way they said it that made the impression.